THE
VALUE OF
PATRIOTISM

THE
VALUE OF
PATRIOTISM
by
Carolyn Simpson

The Rosen Publishing Group, Inc.
New York

Published in 1993 by The Rosen Publishing Group, Inc.
29 East 21st Street, New York, NY 10010

First Edition

Photo research by Vera Ahmadzadeh

Library of Congress Cataloging-in-Publication Data

Simpson, Carolyn
    The value of patriotism / by Carolyn Simpson. — 1st ed.
        p.   cm.
    Includes bibliographical references and index.
    Summary: Explores the nature of patriotism and how it may be expressed in wartime and in different countries and cultures.
    ISBN 0-8239-1288-4
    1. Patriotism—Juvenile literature. [1. Patriotism.] I. Title.
JC329.S56   1993
323.6'5—dc20   93-21961
                                                               CIP
                                                               AC

Manufactured in the United States of America

About the Author

Carolyn Simpson is an adjunct instructor in Psychology at Tulsa Junior College, Tulsa, Oklahoma. She received a bachelor's degree in Sociology from Colby College in Waterville, Maine, and a master's in Human Relations from the University of Oklahoma.

She has worked as a clinical social worker in both Oklahoma and Maine, and as a counselor/instructor in an alternative high school program in Bridgton, Maine.

Other books she has written for young adults include *Coping With an Unplanned Pregnancy, Coping With Emotional Disorders*, and *Careers in Social Work*. She lives with her husband and three children, and assorted pets, on the outskirts of Tulsa.

ACKNOWLEDGMENTS

I cannot claim to have written this book alone. Oh, sure; I was the one surrounded by a stack of library books, and I was the one to sit alone in front of this word processor. But several people gave me ideas, probed me with questions, and shared their own thoughts on patriotism. I'd like to thank them here.

Thanks to all those who helped make my book better, especially my parents, Clifton and Nellie Clarke, who reconstructed their experiences with World War II for me. To Tom Clote, who gave me insight into environmental problems and owns the most complete set of *Utne Readers*. To Steve Hardersen, who defined military changes for me, and to Vickie Hemken, who was willing to risk her life in the service of her country. To Philip Simpson, who shared his ideas on patriotism and thoughts on the American wars, and to Lou Ann for encouraging me to write this book in the first place.

A special thanks to the women in the Tulsa City County Library—especially my friends in the Broken Arrow branch— for helping me find books and people I couldn't seem to find on my own. And to my friends at Little Professor Bookstore, who supplied me with many of my resources. To Ruth Rosen who first suggested this topic and then went on to supply me with details and support.

Most of all, I thank my husband, Dwain, who was a good sport for listening to my ideas—and sharing his own—sometimes into the wee hours of the morning.

The photographs in this book are courtesy of AP/Wide World Photos.

Contents

PART I

THE VALUE OF PATRIOTISM

CHAPTER 1

Who Are the Patriots?

The American Revolution had been dragging on for three years, with few engagements and much suffering. Some women followed their husbands into battle. Molly Pitcher was one of them. During the Battle of Monmouth, she fetched water for the hot and tired soldiers. Amid bullets and musket balls, she ran back and forth to a creek, hauling water for the men. When her husband died loading the cannon, Molly took up his position and kept the big gun firing. At one point, a bullet tore through her petticoat and between her legs. "Good thing it wasn't any higher," she said, and continued to stoke the cannon while the battle raged on.

During the Gulf War in 1991, General Norman Schwarzkopf of the American forces said flatly, "None of us wants to die, but there are certain things out there worth fighting for. I would die for my family tomorrow, to protect my family. And I think freedom, liberty . . . are some things you have to be willing to die for."

The value of patriotism is very clear. Some people who are willing to risk their lives ensure that the rest of us live better

lives. The freedoms that people in many countries take for granted (the right to own property, to marry or not, to receive an education, to vote) were fought for by everyday people. Humankind was not blessed with all these rights at the dawn of civilization. Men and women struggled in every country to secure them and are still struggling today. We owe those people much.

Patriots love their country, and because of that love they are willing to die for it. Patriots commit themselves to an ideal—usually freedom—and do "what it takes" to achieve or to hang onto it. That is good. Without risk-takers, without fighters, we would have little change. Patriots are heroes, then. Or are they all?

What if a patriot believes in an immoral cause? What if he or she behaves immorally to achieve a moral end? When, if ever, is patriotism wrong? Think back to when you were a child. How did you know which characters on television were the good guys and which were the bad guys? It was easy enough then: The good guys always won. As you get older, the rules seem to change. It becomes harder to tell the good guys from the bad because the good guys don't always win anymore. Besides that, the good guys are not always the more appealing. And further, sometimes the bad guys turn out to be good enough guys underneath. What a dilemma!

Is patriotism moral? Is there a connection between the ideal to which you are committed and its benefit to mankind? If you know the answer, you know whether or not you think terrorists are patriotic, whether or not the Ku Klux Klan is inspired by patriotism, and whether or not Oliver North was a patriot for selling arms to Iran in exchange for hostages.

Does patriotism mean blind allegiance to your country? Does it mean "My country, right or wrong"? The Japanese kamikazes were members of suicide squadrons who willingly killed themselves for their country because they were trained

General H. Norman Schwarzkopf, successful commander of U.S. forces in the Persian Gulf, gives the crowd a "thumbs up" during a Welcome Home ticker tape parade.

to do so. The Nazi party believed that Hitler *was* Germany, and whatever order he gave them, they obeyed to serve their country. During the Vietman War, thousands of young men and women protested the draft. They were not willing to fight and die in a war they believed was wrong. Does that make the Nazis, not the student protesters, patriots?

Can a person be a patriot if he or she objects to violence? Does refusal to fight, even in a declared war, make a person unpatriotic? You can support your country in many ways, even if you are unwilling to take up arms. Some people opted for community service during the Vietnam draft; some people entered the war only as doctors, nurses, and chaplains. Furthermore, some people never endorsed violence as a way to achieve their ideal. Mohandas Gandhi used nonviolent means to win India's independence in 1947; Martin Luther King used nonviolent means (protests, marches, strikes) to seek equality for all peoples. Were they any less patriotic for not taking up arms?

And just what is your country anyway? Is it the nation to which you owe your allegiance, or is it the whole earth? With the world having shrunk because of improved communications, how can we not be affected by what happens in other states or countries? Does that make environmentalists patriotic even if they disrupt other people's ways of life?

Clearly, understanding patriotism is not such an easy matter. Issues of right and wrong change the picture. When is a patriot really a zealot, someone who fanatically pursues his own ideals? When is he acting in self-interest? What are the risks a patriot assumes? What are the risks to those who love him or her and who live with him or her? Those are some of the questions this book tries to answer.

For the moment, who pops into your mind at the mention of patriots? Do you think of Paul Revere, who risked his life riding past the British to warn Samuel Adams and John Hancock? Do you think of George Washington, who rallied his troops during battle and on many occasions braved the front lines to encourage them? Do you think of Abraham Lincoln, who risked the wrath of the American public to preserve his country? Naturally, these heroes spring to mind because their deeds were so courageous and inspiring. But patriots can also

The crew of the U.S. space shuttle Challenger lost their lives when the shuttle exploded shortly after liftoff in January 1986.

be the common people who do what it takes to keep going. Let's consider some unusual patriots, who were heroic all the same.

In 1982, ten-year-old Samantha Smith in Manchester, Maine, was worried about the possibility of nuclear war, so she wrote a letter to Yuri Andropov, then General Secretary of the Central Committee of the Communist Party of the U.S.S.R. She simply asked him if he wanted war and told him how she felt. That in itself was a brave and poignant gesture, but the story did not end there. Andropov wrote back and invited

Samantha to visit the Soviet Union as his guest, to meet the people and see for herself what they were like. Samantha Smith, with her parents, flew to the Soviet Union and spent two weeks touring the country and spreading goodwill. The Soviet people were so impressed that they created a stamp to honor her. Many Americans consider this little girl a patriot.

In August 1991, the Soviet military and agents of the Communist Party tried to overthrow President Mikhail Gorbachev. While he was held prisoner at his vacation home outside Moscow, tanks moved into Moscow to capture the Russian White House. Boris Yeltsin stood his ground and ordered the tanks to "go home." The Russian people, in a heroic show of support for their leader, climbed onto the tanks to prevent their movement. Newspapers captured pictures, not only of men climbing the tanks, but of women who braved gunfire to protect their leader. In the end, the Soviet coup was thwarted by the Russian people themselves.

Until January 28, 1986, not many people thought about the danger astronauts face in rocketing off into space. Until that day there had never been a disaster on liftoff. On that day, the U.S. space shuttle Challenger blew up, killing all on board, including an elementary school teacher who was to have been the first teacher in space. Most of the country saw the explosion, as it was played over and over again by the media. It was only then that many people realized the courage it takes to climb aboard a "four-million-pound aluminum and ceramic tile flying machine powered by dangerous propellants." Were all the astronauts and cosmonauts patriots? Did they fly because they loved their country or because they wanted to be among the first to experience outer space? Does their spirit of adventure make them any less patriotic?

Men and women around America are trying to take back their streets. If the police and government cannot keep the drug dealers out of their neighborhoods, the residents will. At the risk of being harassed and killed themselves, they attempt to drive the drug dealers out. These ordinary citizens do not profess to be patriots; they just want a safe environment for their children, and they are willing to fight for one. To be willing to risk your life for the betterment of others and in defense of liberty—is that not the definition of a patriot?

With the next two examples, you will see that patriots are equally fervent on both sides of an issue. How to decide which one is right? Actually, there are not always good guys and bad guys on an issue. In this situation there are two good guys with opposing viewpoints on the Middle East question of a Jewish and a Palestinian homeland. How the world will help to settle this question remains to be seen.

Golda Meir, who was born in Russia and fled to America, made Palestine her homeland in 1921. Palestine was then ruled by the British, who had wrested it from the Ottoman Empire. Jews wanted to make it their home; Arabs objected. Golda Meir immersed herself in the fight for a Jewish state. Great Britain was not willing to relinquish its hold on Palestine, and out of concern for the Arab population (who greatly out-numbered the Jews) began to restrain Jewish immigration. Knowing the dangers for Jews in Europe during World War II, Golda Meir worked even harder for their independence and to open the doors to any Jew who wanted to immigrate there. In 1947 Britain agreed to partition Palestine into Jewish and Arab sections. Then, because war was imminent with the surrounding Arab nations that opposed Israel, Golda Meir went to the United States to seek donations to fund such a war. In six weeks she raised $50 million for the cause. The Israelis prevailed in war and the State of Israel was created in 1948. Golda Meir eventually became prime minister; for many years she protected the rights of her people until her death in 1978.

Hanan Ashrawi is a Palestinian wife, mother, and college professor. She lives and teaches in the West Bank, which is the Arab portion of Palestine occupied by the Israelis. She supports the Palestine Liberation Organization (PLO), which still lacks a homeland. Hanan Ashrawi calls for Israel to leave the West Bank and Gaza for "humanitarian reasons." She has been instrumental in pleading the Palestinian cause on U.S. radio and television, particularly after the Intifada of 1987

when the Palestinians in the occupied areas began to fight back at the Israelis. Ironically, she wants the same thing for her people that Golda Meir wanted for hers: a homeland. Both peoples feel entitled to the land. The Israelis believe they have biblical ties to the land that outweigh anything else. The Palestinians believe that they had Palestine first and should not be pushed aside to make a homeland for the Jews with their radically different religious beliefs. As of 1993 no compromise has been acceptable to both sides. Periodic wars have been fought over the right to these territories. Following the Gulf War in 1991, the Israelis and their Arab neighbors agreed to sit down for peace talks, but so far the talks have produced only stalemate. Hanan Ashrawi was arrested and detained for having addressed a meeting of the PLO to seek their support; it is against the law to meet with the PLO if you reside in Israel. She continues to serve as a mediator. She said in 1991, "I refuse to be intimidated and I refuse to be silenced." In that respect, she and Golda Meir are very much alike.

Hanan Ashrawi is a patriot fighting for a Palestinian homeland.

CHAPTER 2

How We Learn About Patriotism

Why is it that some people are patriotic and others seem to have no regard for their country? Are people born that way? Or do life experiences shape them?

Whether people are born inherently good or bad is a question that philosophers have pondered for years. I prefer to believe that we all start out good, or at least, neutral, which then leaves us open to be shaped by life experiences. One is not born a patriot, but one can grow up to be patriotic, especially if shaped by positive forces.

Your first glimpse of life is through the eyes of your family. There you can learn about love, commitment, and responsibility. If you are raised to feel good about yourself and your environment, to believe that you can have a positive effect on the world, you will have pride in yourself and a sense of duty to your country. Your parents and grandparents may have told you bedtime stories about heroes. Relatives who fought in wars may have talked about their experiences, or you may have picked up on their patriotism when you heard their feelings about war in general. Families may not set out to make their members patriotic per se, but by instilling a sense of loyalty, respect for the work ethic, belief in fairness, and appreciation for our freedoms, they *teach* us to be patriotic. Of course, they teach best by example.

Patriotism is learned in school and church. In the United States, students recite the Pledge of Allegiance every morning before class. In Japan or any Communist country schoolwork is tied to love of country. Students learn about duty and honor as well as the lessons of math and science.

The flag probably hangs in every classroom, and you learned to recognize your country's flag by the time you were five or six. You learned how to treat the flag—that a flag dragged through the dirt or displayed upside down (unless as a distress signal) is a sign of dishonor. Without really knowing why, you may even get teary when you hear the national anthem played, even if you don't fully understand the words or the meaning behind the words.

If history is not your favorite subject, you are not alone. Some people see no point in reading about things that happened long ago. But think a little further. First of all, we all need to know how our country began and its relationship with other countries. To understand a country's history and culture is to understand its people. After all, we are all products of our past.

For another thing, history has a way of repeating itself.

Some countries indoctrinate students with the idea of duty and obedience to country above all else. Early in the twentieth century, Japanese students were trained to be loyal subjects, willing to do whatever the Emperor demanded of them. Teachers instilled unquestioning love of country in their students. The same thing happened in Nazi Germany. Children learned the lessons Hitler wanted them to learn to support a fanatical devotion to his ideals. Beginning in 1979, the same thing occurred in Iraq. The president, Saddam Hussein, restructured the educational system to reflect his version of history. Students are taught that Saddam Hussein is a direct descendant of the prophet of Allah, the Islamic god, Muhammad, and therefore rules by divine power. Thus, they owe allegiance equally to Muhammad and Hussein.

As you can see, schools are an important source of patriotism, and not simply because of the classwork. Most of us learn school pride before we learn community pride. We

Once a symbol of Communist glory, the statue of Vladimir Lenin is toppled by angry Soviet people in 1990.

identify with a school, we participate in the band or in sports, we learn the school song; we support our team against the rival school. We learn about team play, sacrificing self for the good of the team. The Olympic Games are an extension of that experience, but there you represent your country, not simply your school and community. Instead of your school banner floating over the scene, your nation's flag is raised. Millions of people are proud of your accomplishments because you represent them, and so they are honored, too.

Patriotism is encouraged on national holidays (usually days of independence: July 4 for the United States, July 1 for Canada, July 14 for France). The parades with patriotic floats and uniformed marchers preceded by the flag are intended to stir your pride. In the United States, Memorial Day honors the dead of all wars and Veterans Day honors all who served in the armed forces.

People learn about patriotism through their country's symbols. The American eagle stands for freedom. Some early Americans wanted to make the turkey the national symbol. Which do you think better projects the image of a free, strong country, the turkey or the eagle? Consider some other symbols. The Statue of Liberty, gift of France to the United States, is another symbol of freedom. For many immigrants, it was their first glimpse of their new land as their ship approached Ellis Island. The Vietnam War Memorial in Washington, D.C., names all the people who died serving the country in the Vietnam War. Because of the controversy surrounding that war, the Memorial has become a symbol of sacrifice and belated recognition.

The black anchor was the symbol of wartime Poland. The rising sun has long been a symbol of Japan, and since World War II it has been associated in the United States with aggression and infamy. The swastika is an ancient symbol of good luck. Since the Nazis adopted it as their party emblem, however, it has been associated with the regime of Adolf Hitler, the very personification of evil.

When the Soviet Union was dismantled in December 1991, and even earlier when communism ended, statues of Lenin and Stalin were torn down by the people. What once had represented glory now represented the totalitarian regime that the Soviet people hated.

Flags, however, are the most notable national symbols. The colors and design all stand for something, often courage and tenacity. The United States Congress did not approve the national flag until 1777. Until then, the British Union Jack or versions of it had been in use. Canada did not devise the maple leaf flag until 1964; like the American colonies, it had used the British flag. During the 1992 Winter Olympics, there was no flag for the Soviet team. The Soviet Union had been dissolved in December 1991. With most of the republics declaring independence, the U.S.S.R. no longer existed. Russians wanted their own flag, as did the other republics. When the Soviet team won a medal, the Olympic flag was raised instead. It was a constant reminder to all how the world had changed.

Last, consider the influence of the media, notably television and movies. Who are the heroes, and what are their ideals? In the 1950s and '60s, Superman fought for "truth, justice, and the American way." The British secret agent 007 taught other lessons as well as love of country, but good always won out over bad. Now we have "Rambo," an ex-soldier who is used by his country to fight the whole world, and "The Terminator." What are the media telling us about patriotism? Who are the people's heroes these days, and what does that tell us about them?

No one begins life wanting to be a patriot. You learn to love your family, your community, and your country. You take pride in them all, and by believing you can make a positive contribution, you are a patriot, waiting to act.

You don't always have to die for your country. You just have to care for it.

PART II

PATRIOTISM IN EXPLORATION AND WARTIME

CHAPTER 3

Exploration and Expansion

Throughout history, people have claimed lands in the name of their country. Some may indeed have been patriots; others have been greedy and power-hungry. Do not accept at face value what people claim to do out of love of country. Consider the following examples.

Alexander the Great was not the first to appropriate other lands for his empire, but he is one of the most famous. Having extended his rule throughout southern Europe and the Middle East, he introduced Greek culture as a better way of life. The Romans did the same thing during their years of empire. They conquered peoples in North Africa, Syria, and Mesopotamia and introduced their culture to these "inferior" peoples. Is it patriotic to subdue another country and make subjects of its people? Does it become "right" if the other people are threatening your way of life? And just what constitutes a threat?

In the fifteenth and sixteenth centuries, explorers added many new lands to their countries. In the beginning, the New World was claimed by England, France, and Spain. John Cabot was the first modern explorer to reach North America, and he claimed the land for England. Columbus claimed the West Indies (which he believed to be in the Eastern Hemisphere) for Spain, although he was Italian. Juan Ponce de Léon led explorers in search of the Fountain of Youth, and in 1513 discovered Florida instead, promptly claiming it for Spain. Hernán Cortés set out to conquer Mexico and found the Aztec empire already there. Impressed by their wealth, he conquered the Aztecs and stole their treasure, appropriating the land and its resources for Spain.

Not to be outdone, the French sent explorers to the New World to gain honor and riches for their country. Jacques Cartier sailed north to what is now Canada, discovered the St. Lawrence River, and set up a wooden cross as a marker. On the cross he wrote, "Long live the King of France."

Explorers searched for a shorter route to the Pacific Ocean. They knew that whoever discovered such a route and claimed the territory would make their country very powerful. By the 1600s, the eastern half of the North American continent had been divided between three countries, despite the claim to ownership of the Native Americans. Many battles and wars were fought over land claims until eventually the English acquired most of the territory.

The African continent also has been subjected to conquest and colonization by various European countries. The Republic of South Africa still is under appropriation. Southern Africa is one of the richest regions on the continent because of its wealth of natural resources: minerals, especially diamonds, and rich farmland. It was also strategically located at the southern tip of the continent. Any country that controlled South Africa would have a strategic base for military operations and an ideal port for trade. The first South Africans were the Bantu-speaking Africans from the interior of Africa, who migrated south in search of better land for farming and grazing. The Dutch, who were also successful explorers, arrived by accident in 1647 when shipwrecked survivors came ashore. Others returned and in 1652 built a fort, claiming the land for the Dutch. They called themselves Afrikaners. Rural people, called Boers in the Afrikaans language, steadily displaced the Bantu-speaking peoples. In 1795, when England and the Netherlands were at war, the British seized South Africa. The Dutch and British never got along, so between

1835 and 1843 about 12,000 Afrikaners left the Cape of Good Hope to build homes further inland. What happened to the Africans was the beginning of apartheid.

Seizing other countries in the name of your own continued well into this century. Japan marched into Korea and China during the 1930s. The Soviet Union and Germany partitioned Poland during World War II, and the Soviet Union went on to subject other Eastern European countries to Communist rule. Iraq took over the neighboring country of Kuwait in 1990, which set off the Persian Gulf War. The United States and the U.S.S.R engaged in a race in space to see which country could first land on the moon. The Soviet Union launched the first artificial satellite, Sputnik I, on October 4, 1957. America launched Explorer I in January 1958. On April 12, 1961, the Soviets sent the first human into space, Yuri A. Gagarin, and on May 5, 1961, America followed with Alan Shepard. President John F. Kennedy promised that the U.S. would land a man on the moon by the end of the decade. He didn't promise to be first, but that was widely accepted as the goal. Eight years later, on July 20, 1969, Neil Armstrong and Edwin (Buzz) Aldrin walked on the moon. They left behind the Stars and Stripes, and while the U.S. did not lay claim to the moon, getting there first certainly bolstered national pride.

The quest to master outer space led to many discoveries and vastly improved our way of life. Satellites let us watch live television programs from all over the world. Probes of other planets increased human knowledge of the universe. Were scientists impelled by patriotism—glory for their country—or by curiosity and adventure? Does one exclude the other?

RESISTANCE TO COLONIZATION

Just as patriotic men sailed into the unknown to explore (and claim) new lands for their countries, patriotic peoples resisted invaders. Is it not just as patriotic to resist in the name of your country as it is to take? As America marks the 500th anniversary of Columbus's "discovery" in 1992, remember that North America had long since been discovered.

Edwin ("Buzz") Aldrin poses for his fellow astronaut Neil Armstrong after placing the American flag on the moon in 1969.

Native Americans were not at all willing to abandon their cultures and their lands. Many resisted, but they were inevitably overwhelmed by the white man's sheer numbers and superior weapons. Some trusted him to honor his treaties, but in the end the white man still took their land and destroyed their way of life. While the conquerors considered them savages, were they not really patriots, fighting to preserve their country?

In the late 1800s, Chief Joseph of the Nez Percé tribe tried to help his people escape to Canada after the white man had taken their land and tried to confine them to a reservation in eastern Oregon. They were caught just forty miles south of the Canadian border, and by then they had lost the will to fight. When he was captured, Chief Joseph said, "I am tired of fighting. Our chiefs are killed . . . The old men are killed . . . It is cold and we have no blankets. The little children are freezing to death . . . My heart is sick and sad. From where the sun now stands, I will fight no more forever."

Chief Joseph was again confined to a reservation, but nowhere near his original home. For the rest of his life, he asked to be returned to the land of his ancestors, but his request was never granted.

Just the name Geronimo inspired fear in white settlers during the 1800s. He was a Chiricahua Apache, whose entire family were butchered by the Mexicans. When Mexican lands were ceded to the United States and the white man moved in, Geronimo resisted the only way he knew, by intimidating and sometimes killing white settlers. He was captured many times and placed on reservations in Arizona, but he escaped over and over, to return to the lands he knew so well. Finally he was exiled, first to Florida and then to Fort Sill, an Army base in southwestern Oklahoma, where he died a captive in 1909.

In Canada, the Métis were a mixed race derived from the intermingling of Indians and French trappers. In 1867 the Canadian confederation threatened the Métis' land in what is now Manitoba. Louis Riel led the Métis in a campaign to save their Red River colony from land-hungry Canadians. In 1870 Riel and the Métis asked the Canadian confederation to

admit the Red River settlement as a new province, guarantee-ing their land rights and the preservation of the French language and the Catholic faith. Despite these guarantees, an uprising took place in the settlement and a white settler was killed. Riel fled across the border to Montana, branded a fugitive by the Canadian government. In 1884 a delegation of Métis found him and told him how the agreements had been broken. White settlers had moved onto their lands, forcing two thirds of the colony to find land elsewhere. The Métis had relocated in Saskatchewan, but the Canadian government sought that land as well.

Riel agreed to return to Canada, even at the risk of his own life, and he led his people in a second resistance, which has been called the Northwest Rebellion. Riel was caught, tried for treason, and hanged. Was Riel a patriot or an outlaw? Could he have been both? To the British Canadians, he was an outlaw; to the French Canadians, he was a hero.

The most important lesson of all these examples is that patriotism can flourish on both sides of an issue. What is praised by one group may be condemned by another. Were the explorers wrong in seeking glory for their country? Were the subjugated peoples wrong for resisting? In the end, both were patriotic when they placed the love and defense of their country ahead of power and greed.

Geronimo, a Chiricahua Apache, fought colonization of the Midwest until he was captured and exiled to Oklahoma, where he died.

CHAPTER 4

The American War for Independence

Wars have always produced heroes and villains. Most people believe that those who willingly fought were the heroes and those who shirked that duty were the villains.

Loving one's country does not always mean fighting for it. There are other ways of demonstrating patriotism, as we shall see in the following examples from the Revolutionary War.

Contrary to popular thinking, the Revolutionary War was not initially fought to gain the colonies' independence from England. When the Boston colonists fired back at the British in Lexington and Concord and urged the other colonies to join in the fight against England, they were trying to oust the British troops from the country. The Americans wanted the same rights that the English had: the right not to be taxed without representation in Parliament, and the right not to have their trade dictated. It was only after the bloody battle of Breed's Hill (commonly called the Battle of Bunker Hill) that the rest of the colonies agreed to separate from England. They did not want to belong to a country that would butcher its own people, colonists or not.

SAMUEL ADAMS

Samuel Adams was arguably the most radical of the patriots. It was his idea to gain independence from Britain from the beginning. He had been provoking the British for a decade, inciting Boston mobs to rebel. Some believe that he stirred up the mob before the Boston Massacre, in which five colonists were shot to death by cornered British soldiers, and that he masterminded the Boston Tea Party. Adams operated behind the scenes; he talked up independence in coffeehouses and fanned the fires of dissent in newspapers. When the British first marched on Lexington and Concord, they were looking to arrest Adams and his colleague, John Hancock, intending to wipe out colonial resistance. Paul Revere succeeded in riding past the British to warn the Boston leaders, although contrary to folklore he did not ride through the countryside awakening the people of Concord. Revere was captured after warning Adams and Hancock. It was Samuel Prescott who rode the rest of the way to Concord to alert the people.

The British considered Samuel Adams a rabblerouser, and from their viewpoint they were right. He did want independence from England, and he was delighted when he provoked their rage. He was never motivated by greed, however, and he remained contentedly poor his whole life. In fact, when he first joined the Continental Congress, the people of Massachusetts bought him clothes and shoes because he owned nothing worthy of the occasion.

Samuel Adams wanted the best for his country. Of course, he chose for himself what that might be. That is where the danger always lies: when one person decides for many what is best. Adams feared the limitless power of the monarchy and wanted more freedom for Americans. Throughout the Revolutionary War, he worried that George Washington had imperial ambitions and believed that any day Washington would crown himself king. Nonetheless, Samuel Adams was the spark that ignited the people.

BENJAMIN FRANKLIN

Benjamin Franklin was another colonial patriot who did not wage war with arms. At seventy-two, he was not in a position to lend the soldiers assistance on the battlefield. However, he believed in the American cause and used his enormous prestige abroad to secure the backing of the French government. Without France, the Americans could not have prevailed against the British. The French sent money (badly needed to purchase arms and supplies for the soldiers), ships, and men like the Marquis de Lafayette, who led American troops in battle.

The French were not eager to support the Americans in a failing cause. They had had enough trouble with England and did not want to risk another war for lending support to a rebellious colony. So it was up to Franklin to convince the French that the Americans could win, and it was up to George Washington to deliver a few victories toward that end. Franklin succeeded in generating their goodwill, and France entered into an alliance with the colonies on February 6, 1778. When the war ended, Benjamin Franklin stayed on in Europe to help draw up the terms of the peace treaty that was signed on September 3, 1783.

JOHN PAUL JONES

John Paul Jones was a naval hero in the Revolutionary War. The French had given him a ship, which he renamed the *Bonhomme Richard*. Without French ships, the colonists would have had no navy to speak of. In 1779, Jones and a squadron of five ships, sailing off the coast of England, encountered a British convoy of forty-one merchant ships and two warships, the *Serapis* and the *Countess of Scarborough*. Jones's force captured the *Countess,* but the *Bonhomme Richard* was getting the worst of it, and the British admiral ordered, "Strike your colors," meaning to furl the flag, or surrender. Jones replied, "I have not yet begun to fight." Pulling alongside, he lashed his ship to the *Serapis* to hamper its firepower. By the end of the moonlit battle, the British fleet had surrendered. Two days later, the *Bonhomme Richard* sank.

GEORGE WASHINGTON

George Washington was a patriot who fought. Although his military strategy has been questioned, no one has ever disputed his courage. Samuel Adams and others were suspicious of his ambitions, but no one could doubt his dedication to his army and his country. The Continental Congress voted George Washington commander of the American army, which at the time was little more than a band of ragtag recruits. Desertions and lack of supplies during the early months took a toll on the army. Washington knew that he was not equipped to take on the vastly superior English troops. His soldiers were not professionally trained, and they had neither the modern weapons nor the ammunition of the enemy. Furthermore, his troops were hungry and footsore.

Washington could have thrown in the towel many times, and history would not have blamed him. Instead, he recruited the soldiers he needed (appealing to their patriotism), and he became a master of retreat in battle. He badly needed a victory to bolster morale—his own, as well as that of his troops. On Christmas Day in 1776, Washington led his troops across the semifrozen Delaware River, and surprised the reveling Hessian troops, quickly capturing the enemy, his supplies, and his weapons. After the battle, Washington appealed to his troops to sign on for six more weeks. His need for them, far more than money or their own desire, persuaded his soldiers to reenlist.

As the war dragged on, until the French sent men and arms, Washington's greatest challenge was keeping his men fed and clothed. He never accepted a salary for this job. Countless times he put his life on the line to rally his troops in battle. Before the Battle of Monmouth, one of his commanders became confused in the unfamiliar terrain. As his men fled in disarray, Washington rode to the front lines and turned the men back. His troops became more fearful for their general, who was riding at their head on a conspicuous

George Washington and his heroic soldiers cross the Delaware River in one of the most critical events of the Revolutionary War.

horse, than for themselves. Washington believed he could do nothing less than what he expected of his troops.

JOHN HANCOCK

John Hancock was a wealthy Bostonian whom Samuel Adams helped convert to the American cause. In the early days, he and Adams were the force behind the struggle for independence. After Paul Revere had alerted them about the advancing British force, Hancock wanted to stay and fight on the Lexington green. Adams had to persuade him that he was more important as a delegate to the Congress than as a soldier.

Hancock was elected president of the Continental Congress, and when the Declaration of Independence was presented for endorsement, he was the first to sign—an act of treason to the British crown. The story arose that John Hancock wrote his name with such a flourish to ensure that he became the number one villain on the British hit list. Supposedly he said, "There! John Bull can read my name without spectacles and may now double his reward of five hundred pounds for my head."

Whether or not Hancock was partly motivated by vainglory, he risked his life in signing the Declaration. Patriots are human beings and hence neither all good nor all bad. Patriotism is sometimes not a black or white matter.

THOMAS PAINE

Thomas Paine, the great pamphleteer of the Revolution, was not even an American by birth. He did not come from England to the colonies until November 1774. For Paine, the pen was indeed mightier than the sword. He urged the colonists on to independence in his pamphlet *Common Sense*. He then signed over the copyright to the Continental Congress, which in essence was a gift of a fortune to the American cause. Unlike Patrick Henry, who could inspire with his oratory, Paine inspired with his prose. Paine served in the Continental Army as a volunteer aide. At nights he wrote a series of pamphlets called *The American Crisis*. Washington was so moved by his words that he had them read to his disheartened troops. The following excerpt from the first of the series shamed some of the men, who were merely biding their time until their enlistment was up: "These are the times that try men's souls. The summer soldier and the sunshine patriot will, in this crisis, shrink from the service of his country; but he that stands it *now*, deserves the love and thanks of man and woman. Tyranny, like hell, is not easily conquered; yet we have this consolation with us, that the harder the conflict, the more glorious the triumph. What we obtain too cheap, we esteem too lightly; 'tis dearness only that gives everything its value. . . ."

To the men who gave Americans their independence—the planners of the war and the new government, the men and women who supported the troops, and those who fought the battles—Americans owe a debt of gratitude. They risked their lives and well-being so that their descendants could live in freedom.

CHAPTER 5

The American Civil War

The American Civil War did for the United States what the Revolutionary War had failed to do: It unified the states into a single, powerful country. The colonists fought and won independence from England, and they organized a government to represent all thirteen states. However, the issue of states' rights was not resolved, and the people's allegiance was first to their state, not the national government.

The Civil War was not fought to abolish slavery. Objections to slavery and the South's fear of losing its way of life sparked feuding among the states. That gave rise to the issue of states' rights. The Southern states feared that the North, with its wealth based on manufacturing, would overpower them; they saw their rights being undermined. If the South remained a part of the Union, it would not be long before the North ran the whole show (or so the thinking went.) Southern states (and Southern gentlemen) could not abide a country where their vote counted for little. If Abraham Lincoln were elected President, they feared, he would tamper with their way of life. So seven Southern states initially seceded from the Union.

The Civil War began because Lincoln wanted to preserve the Union. When the war ended, the people realized for the

first time that the Union was more than the sum of the individual states and that any state that left the Union would weaken it. Lincoln made it very clear that slavery was not the cause of his entering the war. He wrote, "My paramount object in this struggle is to save the Union, and is not either to save or to destroy slavery. If I could save the Union without freeing any slave, I would do it; and if I could do it by freeing all the slaves, I would do it; and if I could save it by freeing some and leaving others alone, I would also do that."

The Civil War created a unified country, but at tremendous cost. It was the most destructive war ever waged by the United States. Some 360,000 Union soldiers lost their lives; 260,000 Confederate soldiers lost theirs. They were fighting other Americans on American soil; in some cases, they were fighting their own brothers, uncles, fathers. Senator John Crittenden sent two sons to the war: One fought for the Union, one for the Confederacy. Abraham Lincoln's brother-in-law joined the Confederacy. Towns and states were divided; some sent regiments to support the North and others to support the South.

All wars are ugly, but the Civil War was particularly horrible. Men fought at close range, firing their weapons into recognizable countrymen. Often they fought hand-to-hand, stabbing and shooting. How much worse to watch a man die who looked no different from you.

Men who survived wounds on the battlefield usually died (or prayed to die) in the field hospitals. The period was the end of the medical Middle Ages. The world did not yet know about germs, sterilization, and antibiotics. The Southern hospitals lacked painkillers, and many men faced amputations without sedatives. The rifles in use fired bullets too powerful for close-range use. Were someone shot in the arm, for example, the arm had to be amputated because the destruction of bone and tissue was too great to repair.

Those whom gunfire and bayonets failed to kill, disease took. Many men died from measles and mumps.

The last photograph of Abraham Lincoln, taken in 1865.

At a Union camp at Gettysburg, a physician prepares to amputate a soldier's leg.

The war produced its share of heroes—not all of them generals. Most were common folk, transformed by acts of patriotism.

WOMEN IN THE WAR

Women played a heroic role in the Civil War. Clara Barton and other women took to the battlefield (sometimes while the battle was raging) as nurses. Clara Barton, who went on to found the American Red Cross, displayed great courage, once helping to steady an operating cart while bullets whizzed around her. Women back home (in both the North and South) managed the homesteads, took care of the crops, entered the factories, sewed uniforms for their men and sent them food. Sanitary Commissions raised money to improve conditions in the army, and sanitary commissioners investigated the army barracks. They provided blankets and made sure that "care packages" were distributed equally among the soldiers. In no small part because of their efforts, disease was halved from what it had been during the Crimean War.

AFRICAN AMERICANS IN THE WAR

African Americans played a role in the Union victory. At first they were not allowed to fight, although Frederick Douglass argued that they had the most reason of all to do so. Southerners did not want their slaves to leave the fields and take up arms, nor did they trust freedmen to support their cause. Lincoln was willing to use black soldiers in the Union army, but he feared that white men would not fight beside them. However, the need for soldiers was so great that Lincoln relented and allowed the formation of all-black regiments (led by white officers). These men risked far more than did their white counterparts; if they were captured, the Confederates would torture and kill them, or sell them into slavery. Nonetheless, blacks enlisted by the hundreds; even the great abolitionist Frederick Douglass sent his two sons to war. He would have enlisted himself, but he was considered too old.

You may have heard of the all-black 54th Massachusetts Regiment, immortalized in the movie "Glory." These soldiers, headed by Colonel Robert Gould Shaw (son of the Boston abolitionist), led a charge against a Southern fort that they knew was destined to fail. By sacrificing themselves, they bought time for the Union troops to arrive behind them. Despite almost certain death, these men chose to fight. When the colorbearer (the man who carried the regiment's banner) fell in battle, Sergeant William Carney rescued the flag despite taking bullets in his head, chest, arm, and leg. Carney was the first of twenty-three African Americans to win the Congressional Medal of Honor.

The movie "Glory" tells the story of the all-black 54th Massachusetts Regiment.

When Confederate soldiers found the body of Colonel Shaw, who had been killed in the charge, they threw it into a mass grave with his black troops. The Confederates meant it as an insult, but Shaw's father believed that no greater tribute could have been given than to bury the commander with his men.

SHERMAN AND LEE

Civil War generals gained reputations both as heroes and villains. General William Tecumseh Sherman broke the Confederates' resistance with his march across Georgia to the sea. He believed that if he destroyed the Confederates' countryside, homes, and farms, he would shorten the war. He did just that, but in the process he ravaged the land and razed the cities. Cheered by the Northerners (including Lincoln), he was vilified by the Southerners, whose back he had broken. Sherman was most assuredly a patriot, but not to the South of his day.

Robert E. Lee of Virginia retained the aura of a gentleman throughout the war, a war he had not wished to pursue. In the beginning, Abraham Lincoln offered him the command of the Union forces. Lee refused; with Virginia one of the states to secede from the Union, he could not take up arms against his own people. Part of the reason the war dragged on so long was the ineptness (and vacillation) of the early Union generals and the brilliance of General Lee. Lee endeared himself to his men, and he conceded defeat at Appomattox only because his men and their families were starving.

ABRAHAM LINCOLN

A discussion of patriotism during the Civil War would be incomplete without mention of Abraham Lincoln. A man of lesser resolve might have let his country break apart. Lincoln knew that his antislavery ideas antagonized the South, and he tried to compromise with both sides—those who wanted to retain slavery (which was the underpinning of the South's cotton trade) and those who wanted to abolish it altogether. Lincoln was willing to tolerate slavery in the South as long as it did not flourish in any new states. Even when he announced the Emancipation Proclamation (to take effect in 1863), he was not abolishing slavery everywhere. He was setting free only the slaves in states that were in open rebellion against the United States. The move was a great stroke of compromise. Slaves in the South considered themselves free, but since the war had yet to be won, they were not exactly free. Foreign countries were no longer willing to come to the aid of the Confederacy because it would be supporting a country that endorsed slavery. Slaves in the border states that supported the Union were not affected—which was as Lincoln wished it; he did not want to jeopardize their continued support. It was not until Congress passed the 13th Amendment to the Constitution in 1865 that slavery was finally, totally abolished.

Lincoln incurred the wrath of the South and many Northerners. He endured the jabs of journalists, who apparently believed they could wage the war better than he. He suffered immeasurably when his young son died during Lincoln's first term, and he continued to suffer as young men (Northern and Southern) died on the battlefield. Lincoln did not even expect to be reelected in 1864 because the country was growing tired of war. Opposed by George McClellan, one of his former generals, he thought the army would support their beloved general. But because of McClellan's confusing stand on the war (he was a Democrat and wanted peace at all costs), the soldiers supported Lincoln overwhelmingly. Many said they didn't want to have fought in vain, and they believed Lincoln would let them finish what they had started.

Lincoln aged decades in the brief years he served as President. The weight of the world, at least the American world, rested on his shoulders. His idealism and goodwill never deserted him, as demonstrated in the generous terms he offered the South at the end of the war. "With malice toward none; with charity for all...," he declared in his second Inaugural Address.

CHAPTER 6
World War II

Patriotism is sometimes confused with nationalism, but the two are hardly alike. Patriots love their country; nationalists take that love one step farther. They esteem their country above any other and attempt to press their culture on others. Alexander the Great and Julius Caesar were nationalists.

Patriotism is not synonymous with greed; nationalism is. Nationalism seeks to set a nation apart from others, even one ethnic group from others. Patriots can and do become zealots in their country's cause, and some patriots can and do blur into nationalists. No arbitrary line separates one from the other; you must decide that for yourself.

World War II produced many more heroes than villains, although the villains were so treacherous that they stood out more. Let's look at the heroes inspired by Hitler's Germany and the Japanese Imperial Army.

In the late 1930s Adolf Hitler quickly conquered Austria, Czechoslovakia, Poland, Norway, and Holland. He took France in 1940, and then set his sights on England. Seizing England, however, meant getting his armies across the English Channel, and the English were certainly not going to make that easy. Hitler chose to rain bombs on England instead, to destroy the

English mothers kiss their children good-bye at the start of an evacuation during World War II.

land and the cities and to break the British resolve. What he did, however, was to inspire the British people to untold acts of heroism. When the bombing of London started, the British sent their children to the country for safety. The Royal Air Force battled the Germans; a million men too old for military service patrolled the coast as the Homeguard; women took to the factories to replace men drafted into the military and served as radar operators and antiaircraft gunners.

Winston Churchill made it abundantly clear that his country-men would not give up and that Hitler was waging a useless war. Churchill defiantly told the House of Commons and the world, "We shall fight...on the seas and oceans, we shall fight...in the air, we shall defend our island, whatever the cost may be, we shall fight on the beaches, we shall fight on the landing grounds, we shall fight in the fields and in the streets, we shall fight in the hills; we shall never surrender."

And they didn't. Hitler tired of the futility and turned his eyes to his eastern border.

Even as World War II began, Hitler and Josef Stalin of the Soviet Union signed a nonaggression pact. Hitler broke his promise. In 1941 his army invaded Russia. Stalin refused to believe that his ally was actually marching into his country, so the Germans initially were undeterred. When Stalin finally realized Hitler's intent, Russia had already been ravaged. The only hope lay in the Russian people's resistance. They would not resist to save Stalin and his Communist dictatorship; "but," as one author noted "Russia—that was something else. [The Russian soldier] loved the Russian land.... It was holy ... his homeland. And for her he'd fight."

Those Russians who stayed in the cities to fight were the heroes in this theater of the war. They dug trenches to trap the greatly feared German panzers (tanks). Some people even threw themselves in front of the panzers to hamper their progress. Even the weather cooperated, as the bitter winter cold broke the Germans' resolve in the battles of Leningrad, Moscow, and Stalingrad. The Russian people were starving. The Germans were plundering and burning their cities and raping their women, but still the Russians resisted. Their determination both frightened and impressed the German soldiers.

At Stalingrad, General Friedrich von Paulus with the German Sixth Army knew he had neither the men nor the equipment to continue against the Russians. He sent word to Hitler that he wanted to withdraw. Hitler's order came back: He was to fight to the last man. Von Paulus certainly could have done that. The Russian winter, combined with the incredible Russian will, would have destroyed every last man, even as it took a similar toll of the Russians. The general had received a direct order from his Führer: DO NOT SURRENDER. One did not disobey a direct command from Hitler. Yet, General von Paulus did just that. He loved his country, but he also loved his soldiers. A patriot has to do what he believes is right. General von Paulus surrendered his army to the Russians because he realized that his "duty as a man outweighed his oath to Hitler."

The United States had wanted to stay out of the war. As long as what the Japanese (who were waging war in the Pacific)

and Hitler were doing did not impact the U.S., it was willing to remain neutral. Pearl Harbor changed all that. On December 7, 1941, the Japanese staged a sneak attack on Pearl Harbor. Much of the U.S. Navy was bottled up in the harbor; planes stood end to end on the runways—sitting ducks for the Japanese bombers. Eight battleships, three destroyers, and three cruisers were put out of action. Two battleships were totally destroyed, including the *Arizona*, which went down with all its men. In all, 2,323 servicemen were killed. America was ready with a vengeance. War was declared the next day. Men rushed into service, their rallying cry, "Remember Pearl Harbor."

The Japanese seriously misjudged the Americans, just as Hitler had misjudged the British. They believed that the destruction of the Pacific Fleet would be so costly and demoralizing that the U.S. would sue for peace. Instead, the Americans went to war.

Like their British counterparts, American women took over the factory jobs. Women and children collected aluminum to be recycled into machine parts; women went without nylons so that the nylon could be used in tires and parachutes. Food was rationed, and supplies were sent overseas to those in the service. The patriots in this war were all the common folk who gladly served their country by giving their lives, their time, and their support of the cause.

Even the countries that fell into Hitler's hands did not give up. Resistance movements appeared in every occupied country. Paris fell to the Germans in June 1940, and Germans took over the French government. Many resistance groups kept alive French hopes that they would once again be free. General Charles de Gaulle went to England, where he established a government-in-exile to continue the resistance efforts. Those who stayed behind spied on the Germans, informed the Resistance, sabotaged the Germans' wiretapping equipment, and risked death to stage an outright siege of the

The Japanese kamikaze pilots sacrificed their lives for their Emperor and their country.

capital. Hitler's last order to the German commander of Paris was to burn the city. Just as Warsaw had been razed in the siege of Poland, Hitler wanted Paris burned to the ground. If he could not hold the city in the face of the Allied invasion, he would ensure that nothing was left of it. Bomb the bridges, bomb the buildings, kill the people, Hitler demanded.

The French Resistance, with the help of the Allies, pushed the Germans out of Paris in August, 1944. General de Gaulle, who had begged the Allies to alter their plans and free Paris early, marched into the city in triumph. A tall, conspicuous man, he did not even duck the bullets meant to make him cower in public.

The kamikaze pilots present an unusual picture of patriotism. The Japanese Imperial Army was one of the most feared armies on earth; their greatest weapon was their willingness to die for their country. Soldiers who believe it is more honorable to die fighting than to surrender will never put down their weapons and fear nothing the enemy can do to them. From childhood, Japanese men were taught obedience and devotion to the Emperor. Even their bodies belonged to the Emperor; it was their duty to become healthy and strong enough to pass the conscription exams so that they could "perform the honorable duty of defending [their] country."

Japanese soldiers were taught absolute loyalty to the Emperor and unhesitating sacrifice. The kamikaze pilots personified these traits. Since the Japanese could not count on outright defeat of the Americans, whose weapons and resources proved superior to theirs, they resorted to self-sacrifice: crashing their planes into the enemy's ships or other targets. It was a last-ditch effort, but if nothing else, it reinforced the legend of the unstoppable Japanese fighting man. Throughout history, patriots have been willing to die for their country, but the kamikazes *embraced* death. Were they patriots, zealots, or misguided puppets? Were the ideals to which they sacrificed their lives worth dying for, and did the kamikazes even know what those ideals were? Is it right or wrong to kill for your country if you don't know the reason behind the order?

CHAPTER 7

Vietnam and Afghanistan

VIETNAM

Americans in general have been reluctant to wage war, and nowhere did they display greater reluctance than in the Vietnam War. Fathers who had willingly fought in the trenches of World War II helped their sons escape the draft twenty years later. Why was this war so different from the others?

For one thing, it was not clear why the United States was fighting this war. Some people believed in the domino theory that when one country fell to communism, others would fall, too. Therefore, America should go to the defense of South Vietnam to prevent the Communist North from taking it over. By containing communism, America would be keeping the world safe for democracy.

Not everyone subscribed to that theory, however. Some held that America had no business meddling in the affairs of a country halfway across the world. Others maintained that it was a war that the U.S. could never win and that would ultimately stagnate the economy.

Who were the heroes of this war? Were they the men who chose to fight or at least chose not to avoid the draft? Or

were they the protesters, who kept probing the American conscience? Could they have been both? One of the saddest results of the war was that the Vietnam veteran was so little appreciated. Because people did not support the war, they did not support the men and women who fought it. There were no parades to come home to, no heroes' welcome. Even worse, there were no jobs for the returning soldiers. No one felt good about having served his country.

Is it patriotic not to fight? Some students claimed conscientious objector status. They agreed to perform community service at home, or to join the service but not bear arms. Other young men doubted that they would be granted C.O. status and fled to Canada instead. Until President Jimmy Carter pardoned them a decade later, they risked arrest if they set foot in the United States. Protesters decried the war and the draft, leading marches and sit-ins. When Nixon extended the war into Cambodia in 1970, American college campuses erupted. Mass strikes across the nation brought the school year to an early end. Militant protesters took over school buildings and destroyed property.

Rank-and-file Americans who believed it was one's duty to fight his country's war protested the sit-ins and strikes as the actions of unpatriotic, pampered intellectuals. These antiprotest protesters carried signs saying, "America: Love it or Leave it!" Each group believed the other was wrong.

It was hard on the soldiers not to have their country solidly behind them, and they themselves were horrified at the kind of war they were waging. Most had never heard of Vietnam and would be hard pressed to identify it on a map. Many could not fathom what they were fighting to preserve. Certainly not the land; they were destroying that with mines and defoliants. Certainly not the way of life; most of the time they were not even sure who the enemy was.

They were often obliged to kill innocent people. Women and children were sometimes rigged with mines; if you trusted every child that came up to you asking for candy, you risked

Despite the warm words of the poster, there was little support for veterans of the Vietnam War.

getting blown up in the ruse. Frustration with a confusing enemy and a war that was dragging on without success led to a massacre at Mylai in March 1968. One hundred five soldiers of Charlie Company, 11th Brigade, American Division, marched into a Vietnamese village they thought contained the enemy. They killed all its occupants: five hundred old men, women, and children. They had not been "the enemy."

It is unimaginable what tortures the prisoner of war must have faced. Although torture is banned under the Geneva Convention, many countries practice it to extract information from the enemy. The United States now recognizes that soldiers may succumb to torture and divulge secrets. Can one be a patriot and say things against one's country under duress. Were prisoners of war patriots? Or were they casualties of war?

Vietnam showed us both the best in the American people and the worst. It was not clear what constituted "the right thing to do." If following orders could lead to a Mylai massacre, were soldiers expected to weigh the merits of every order? When some people believed it was their duty to fight in an unpopular war, should others have held it against them? When is it your duty to protest a course your country is taking that you believe is wrong?

AFGHANISTAN

Afghanistan was to the U.S.S.R. what Vietnam was to the United States. In 1979 the Soviet Union entered Afghanistan, ostensibly responding to that country's call for help. Rebels had tried to take over the Afghan government, and Soviet troops marched in to protect a hand-picked leader.

As some countries had accused the United States of trying to install its own government in South Vietnam, so people decried the Soviet march into Afghanistan. Some 85,000 Soviet troops were initially sent in, and two thirds of the

This Vietnamese boy survived the massacre at Mylai by hiding under dead bodies.

Afghan army disappeared into the hills. Guerrilla fighting kept the Soviets from putting down roots, while the rest of the world condemned the invasion.

In all likelihood, the Soviet Union wanted control of Afghanistan for political reasons. Nestled in the Middle East, it was much closer to the Persian Gulf, an area to which they had no access. Nonetheless, the Soviets were unable to dominate; the guerrillas resisted, and economic sanctions against the Soviet Union took a toll. The Soviet people were not interested in pursuing this war any more than Americans had been invested in Vietnam. It was costly, and the Soviet people were tired of sending their men and boys off to be killed. Finally, in 1989 the U.S.S.R. withdrew from Afghanistan, leaving the country to solve its own problems minus the threat of Soviet domination.

The major lesson of these countries' experiences is that not all wars are just. It can be equally patriotic to object to your country's involvement as to take up arms. Some wars are waged for the wrong reasons, and it is not unpatriotic to point it out. In a democracy, it is your right to do so.

CHAPTER 8

The Gulf War

The Gulf War of 1991 accomplished two things beyond its stated goal of ousting Saddam Hussein from Kuwait: It united much of the world in a "just" cause, and it reawakened America's pride in its fighting forces.

The war in the Persian Gulf occurred almost two decades after the last American troops left Vietnam. This war was different from Vietnam in every possible way. For one thing, the United States was not trying to settle a country's internal affairs. It headed a thirty-three-nation military coalition, including much of the Arab world. Second, the United States had the endorsement of the United Nations, which had tried economic sanctions unsuccessfully. But most significant, the world largely recognized that this was "a just war" and Americans were right to be there.

In August 1990, Saddam Hussein invaded the oil-rich country of Kuwait. Hussein, the president of neighboring Iraq, claimed that Kuwait had always belonged to Iraq, and he was retaking his "19th province." Despite his protestations to the contrary, most people realized that Hussein was principally interested in the Kuwaiti oil wells. Although tiny compared to nearby Iraq and Iran, Kuwait sits on top of a large portion of the

Saddam Hussein and his son, Odish, in 1990.

world's oil. Were Hussein to absorb Kuwait and its 950 oil wells, he would control 20 percent of the production of the OPEC (Organization of Petroleum Exporting Countries) cartel and 25 percent of world oil reserves. He would be in a position to resume his war with Iran, perhaps to seize the oil kingdom of Saudi Arabia, and then to intimidate Western countries with his hold on oil production.

Saddam Hussein gave the world an even greater reason to fear him: A ruthless dictator, he had slaughtered his own people, the Kurds in northern Iraq, whom he suspected of plotting independence. His army rained chemical gases onto their villages, killing thousands of men, women, and children. He purged members of his own council whenever he suspected disloyalty, and he had videos made of the purges to discourage other possible attempts on his life. The President of the United States, George Bush, likened Saddam Hussein to Hitler, who exterminated millions of his own people in the 1940s. If Hussein were not stopped in Kuwait, he might move against other countries and become unstoppable.

The United Nations agreed that Hussein must be driven from Kuwait, and when economic sanctions failed to move him, it authorized a military force. A metaphorical line was drawn in the sand, and Hussein was ordered to withdraw from Kuwait or face expulsion by force. The U.N. gave him until January 15, 1991. In the meantime, thirty-three nations sent troops, led by the U.S., to Saudi Arabia to await his decision.

The Gulf War, then, was a "just" war, and Americans stood behind their soldiers. Troops started arriving in Saudi Arabia in 1990 as part of a defensive mission, called Desert Shield. France and England sent troops. Japan and Germany, constitutionally barred from sending armies, promised financial support. The Arab countries that did not side with the U.N. forces promised to remain neutral as long as Israel did not participate. No Arab country would tolerate hostile action by the Jewish state against another Arab country.

General Norman Schwarzkopf well remembered Vietnam and was not about to repeat its mistakes. He made the mission clear both to the public and to the soldiers—to oust the Iraqi dictator from Kuwait—and he realized that it must be accomplished in months, not years. The American people would not maintain their enthusiastic backing if their sons and daughters began coming back in flag-draped coffins.

General Schwarzkopf ordered daily bombing missions beginning January 16. Air attacks kept the casualty numbers down and battered Hussein's air defenses and offensive installations. Americans, although shocked at the television reports of actual missions, were buoyed by their apparent ease and success. The allied forces were also upbeat about the mission. General Schwarzkopf had told them prior to waging war, "Our cause is just! Now you must be the thunder and lightning of Desert Storm." One fights to preserve freedom and vital economic interests, and these troops were doing both. The armies were motivated and the people at home were supportive.

While the U.N. forces gathered in Saudi Arabia, planned their strategy, and waited for the deadline to expire, the Kuwaitis resisted. Iraqi forces had stolen their land, looted their buildings, and terrorized their women. The Kuwaiti women, however, protected those in the resistance movement and made life difficult for the invaders. The Palestinians—the largest foreign group living in Kuwait—were torn between allegiance to Kuwait and to the more powerful Saddam Hussein. Those who stayed on to defend Kuwait were nevertheless treated as traitors by the Kuwaitis after the war, and all Palestinians were later deemed "the enemy" because the Palestine Liberation Organization had supported Hussein against Kuwait.

Who were the patriots of the Gulf War? General Norman Schwarzkopf was certainly one. Not only did he mastermind the battle plan that ousted the Iraqis in only six weeks, but he also wove together a force of thirty-three nations, with equal respect for each participating country and its culture. As *Newsweek* noted, General Schwarzkopf was a "man of conscience." He had once remarked that if it ever came to a choice between compromising his moral principles and per-

Nurse Martha Tsuru is reunited with her family upon returning from the Persian Gulf.

forming his duties, he would resign his commission, hang up his uniform, and go with his principles.

Schwarzkopf and his troops restored American pride in their forces. The soldiers returned to a grateful country. Yellow ribbons hung everywhere, symbols of love and appreciation. American flags graced yards and businesses, and miniature versions decorated the helmets of some sport teams. Soldiers returned to parades and welcome-home speeches.

The American troops were clearly patriots, and like all patriots paid a price for their dedication to a cause. Many of those sent to the Gulf were reservists who had full-time jobs and families to support. Some of them had never expected to serve more than a weekend a month and two weeks in the summer. Nevertheless, they left families, new marriages, jobs, and ways of life to board planes and ships bound for the Gulf. Some lost money, others a semester or two of school. Some marriages fell apart while spouses were fulfilling their "duty to their country." Some women had to leave young children in someone else's care while they went off to war. Several women had recently given birth and would not see their babies' first teeth or steps.

The greatest price one pays in the defense of country is one's life. By the end of the war in March 1991, the Pentagon recorded 153 American deaths, 34 people missing in action, and 9 prisoners of war. For a war fought with more than 500,000 U.S. men and women, those figures were remarkably small.

Though Saddam Hussein remains a threat in the Middle East, his regime received a mighty setback. In this case, perhaps the end did justify the means.

PART III

SPIES, TRAITORS, AND QUESTION- ABLE ACTS

CHAPTER 9

Traitors or Patriots?

Let's look at some questionable acts and consider whether or not they can be labeled patriotic. If we condone *some* acts of spying and deceit done for love of country, at what point do we condone mere deceit?

BENEDICT ARNOLD

The case of the most famous American traitor, Benedict Arnold, shows how quickly good can turn bad when greed and power are involved. Arnold did not start out a traitor to his country. In fact, he was an able soldier who served under George Washington during the American Revolutionary War. He helped lead the charge on the British at Fort Ticonderoga. He led an expedition through the Maine wilderness to launch a surprise attack on Canada. He fought in the first battle of Saratoga, a victory that gave the Americans the incentive to continue the war.

Nonetheless, Benedict Arnold had a fatal flaw: arrogance. Arnold wanted to command, not take orders. He was also headstrong; sometimes it was difficult to rein him in. Having been passed over for promotion, he nursed a grudge against the Congress, and only Washington's intervention kept him from resigning.

In the second battle of Saratoga, he galloped into the fray despite orders to stay out. He fought heroically, however, and was instrumental in the victory. His horse was shot out from under him, and he suffered a broken leg. For his services, he was restored to his proper rank.

Washington gave Arnold the military command in Philadelphia, where he could recuperate. There he made friends with Loyalists (the daughter of one of whom he married), and was accused of engaging in profiteering. Apparently he used army wagons to carry commercial supplies that he sold for profit; because he paid the army for use of the wagons, he did not consider his actions criminal. A court-martial convicted him, however, and sentenced him to be reprimanded by General Washington. The General did so with reluctance, but Arnold's disaffection grew, and some months later he made secret contact with the British, offering to change sides. Seeking to gain a more advantageous post to give to the enemy, Arnold asked for and received appointment to the fort at West Point.

The British Major John André, while serving as a go-between for Arnold in the surrender of the fort, was captured by American forces (and later hanged as a spy). Arnold escaped to the British and lived to lead attacks against American forces in the southern colonies. After the war he settled in Canada, disappointed at the lack of recognition he had received in England.

Benedict Arnold began as a patriot, but disaffection and lust for power overcame his loyalty to his country. Like many traitors, he betrayed his country for money and revenge.

JONATHAN POLLARD

The American Jonathan Jay Pollard offers another view of the patriot turned traitor. Although his actions were certainly traitorous, he considered himself a patriot. Devoted to Israel, he spent eighteen months spying on the United States and sold hundreds of classified documents to the Israelis for $45,000 cash. Convicted, he was sentenced in 1986 to life imprisonment. One may question whether allegiance to Israel or cold cash enabled Pollard to rationalize his betrayal of his country. Believing you serve a greater cause can help soften the sense of guilt.

SPY AGENCIES

There are spies in every war; many battles are won because of information gleaned from the enemy. The CIA, the KGB, and the Mossad are government agencies established to supply intelligence on other countries and information on internal dangers. The Central Intelligency Agency is America's vast spy agency "largely funded through a secret Black budget hidden within the Pentagon's overall allocation" of resources. It employs 25,000 people, a handful compared to the former strength of the KGB, its Soviet equivalent. Before the dissolution of the U.S.S.R. and the dismantling of the secret police, the KGB employed 250,000 men and women worldwide.

The Mossad does not offically exist in Israel. The government denies that there is such an agency. Nonetheless, this nonexistent, highly effective secret service employs 1,200 people. The Mossad has been used to combat terrorism in Israel, such as when it hunted down and killed the Arab terrorists responsible for massacring the Israeli athletes at the 1972 Olympics, and elsewhere, as when it supplied information on the hijackers of the luxury liner *Achille Lauro*.

The government agencies are supposed to defend their countries, so their employees should be proud of their work. But what happens in secrecy if the rules are ignored? Sir William Stephenson notes the problem: " . . . Intelligence is an essential weapon. . . . But it is, being secret, the most dangerous. Safeguards to prevent its abuse must be devised, revised and rigidly applied."

Who monitors the secret agencies? Not the journalists, not Ralph Nader, and certainly not the undiscerning public. We

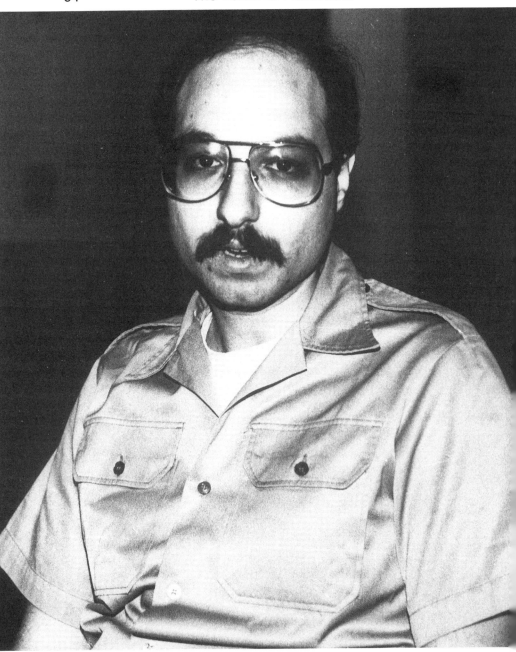

are left to trust that they are doing their jobs. Until we hear otherwise.

How much covert activity is acceptable? It is one thing to spy on a country; it is quite another to intervene in its government (rigging elections, plotting assassinations). Remember the television show "Mission Impossible"? The plots were fiction, but where do you think the writers got their ideas? When is it right to kill for your country? Is it acceptable to commit an immoral act for a moral reason? Who decides what is moral or immoral?

Victor Ostrovsky, author of *By Way of Deception*, a book on the Mossad, raises the question of what happens "when you take a group of highly competitive people and throw away the rules of civilized behavior?" Think about it. What happens when you're a member of a secret organization that has license to do illegal things in the interests of the country it represents? Do you hold onto your principles, or do you succumb to the temptations of money and ego?

On the other hand, what if we did not have these organizations? How would we be able to assess the situation in the Middle East? How would we discover coups before they happened or thwart terrorism? Just as weather satellites can give advance warning of storms, so can secret agencies warn of dangers from abroad or within. The problem lies in who defines what is in the best interests of a nation.

THE IRAN-CONTRA AFFAIR

The United States government had a problem in 1985. Terrorists in the Middle East were kidnapping American journalists and businessmen, including William Buckley of the CIA, who happened to be working in the Middle East at the time. President Ronald Reagan declared that he would not deal with terrorists under any circumstances. The

Jonathan Jay Pollard, a former U.S. Naval Intelligence analyst, was convicted of spying and selling information regarding the U.S. to Israel.

American people demanded the release of the hostages, but their demands went unheeded. At the same time, Iran was embroiled in a bitter war with Iraq. Because the Ayatollah Khomeini had cut off all trade with the United States and other Western countries, Iran was short of arms and other supplies. Reagan's administration—and perhaps Reagan himself, although that has not been proved—decided to sell arms to Iran in exchange for their help in freeing the hostages held in Lebanon. The Iranians denied responsibility for the kidnappings but conceded that they had significant influence over the kidnappers. The problem, however, was Reagan's explicit statement, "No arms for hostages." How could America then sell arms to Iran, which little more than fifteen years earlier had seized the American embassy and held its staff hostage for 440 torturous days?

Clearly, the Reagan administration could not sell arms openly. Therefore, the National Security Council took over the task, and did so covertly. Oliver North was ordered to set up secret deals, and he complied enthusiastically, believing that he was acting in the best interests of his country. Gaining release of the hostages, particularly William Buckley, was "the right thing to do." Selling arms to Iran through Israeli middle-men was not an evil deed because the United States had conflicting views about affairs in the Middle East. Helping to equalize Iran's fight with Iraq was not contrary to American interests.

At every point, Oliver North believed he was following his principles as well as orders, although he recognized that the average American might believe he had circumvented the government. The deals failed to pan out at first, perhaps because Iran and Israel were so distrustful of each other and fearful of political embarrassment should the complicity be discovered.

Defining patriotism and what is right is a difficult task. Lt. Col. Oliver North testifies before the joint Senate-House committee investigating the Iran-contra affair.

While the Iran initiative was in the works, North was asked to find a way to help the contras in Central America. The contras were rebels trying to overthrow the Communist Sandinista government of Nicaragua. The contras needed weapons, supplies, and military guidance. North believed in their cause: They were fighting Communists. Neither the American public nor Congress, however, wanted to arm the contras or be involved in any more of Nicaragua's internal affairs. Congress passed a series of so-called Boland amendments, beginning in 1982, to define and limit what aid could be given the contras. Circumventing the amendments, North enlisted private donors and arranged for military guidance for the contras until the CIA could once again be involved with the approval of Congress.

Then someone involved in the Iran initiative suggested that as long as North was selling arms to Iran, why not sell them for a sizable profit and give that profit to the contras? The United States would be paid for the weapons, Iran would get the arms it needed to continue the war with Iraq, the hostages would be freed, and the contras would benefit.

When actions conflict with acceptable behavior, one often resorts to rationalization to justify one's course. North believed he was operating in his country's best interests. He was following orders from the Reagan administration, if not Reagan himself, and he was acting out of love of country. Does that make Oliver North a patriot? Was it right to undertake these missions without the knowledge and approval of Congress, which was created to keep the President from assuming an imperial role in government?

The Iran-contra affair is still a topic of debate. Oliver North was sentenced to community service; Reagan cannot remember what he knew or didn't know about either operation and has not been prosecuted; former National Security Adviser Robert McFarland was sentenced to community service; and in 1992 former Secretary of Defense Caspar W. Weinberger was under investigation. Before leaving office in 1993, President George Bush pardoned all persons involved in the matter.

Iran-contra raises some moral questions related to patriotism. By whose authority does one do business with terrorists? Who is in charge of government—the President or Prime Minister, or the Congress or Parliament? Is one obligated to follow every order given by a superior? Again, just what role do principles play in determining one's course of action? What gives an individual the right to make decisions for the rest of his country?

The 19th-century reformer Frances Wright, the first woman to give a public Independence Day address, spoke of patriotism: "Patriot is employed to signify a lover of human liberty and human improvement rather than a mere lover of the country in which he lives, or the tribe to which he belongs. Used in this sense, patriotism is a virtue, and a patriot is a virtuous man."

Spying and breaking rules can be ways to safeguard one's country, but what happens when they become a way of life?

CHAPTER 10

Protesters and Dissidents

Henry David Thoreau wrote in *Civil Disobedience*, "Unjust laws exist; shall we be content to obey them, or shall we endeavor to amend them...?" and ever since, people have used him as their guide for disobeying.

Some people protest government policies for the sake of protesting. Not surprisingly, people who have trouble with authority figures are often drawn to the center of any social fracas. Some scuffle with the police simply because they enjoy "acting out." For them, there's nothing like a "good cause" to rationalize attacking the government and its representatives.

Do people have a right to protest their government? And can any "good" come from protesting? Let's look at those men and women who loved their country but believed they needed to speak out to make their country better.

JANE ADDAMS

Jane Addams protested the action of the American government in a productive way. She founded Hull House in Chicago to assist the integration of immigrants into the United States. She established a day-care facility so that mothers could work outside the home, and she taught English and hosted get-togethers so that immigrants could learn— and practice— American customs. In addition, she shared her food with them and taught them better nutrition. Jane Addams was revered for her efforts to improve the conditions of the inner cities. Her Woman's Peace Party, however, brought down on her the wrath of the American people. Jane Addams formed the party in January 1915. Before the United States entered World War I, she urged economic sanctions instead of war. When people called her unpatriotic, she replied, "There [has] to be a better way to show love for your country than dying in a trench."

Although Jane Addams continued to be outspoken on the issue of war, she was very supportive of her country once war was declared. She joined Herbert Hoover's Food Administration, which provided food and medicines to people in the wartorn countries, although many Americans resented her assisting German children. She was elected president of the Women's International League for Peace and Freedom and held that office until 1929. Despite the public view of her wartime activities, Jane Addams was awarded the Nobel Peace Prize in 1931.

STUDENT WAR PROTESTERS

The Vietnam War era brought out a more vociferous group of protesters. Contrary to some opinions, these were not all drug-crazed hippies trying to make the American government look bad. College students, professors, and some governmental officials believed the war was wrong and the United States was wrong to keep pursuing it. Protests took the form of the burning of draft cards and the staging of sit-ins and marches to the ubiquitous chant of "Hell, no! We won't go!". Some people enraged the general public by burning the American flag in an era when that was illegal. In 1990 the U.S. Supreme Court ruled the 1989 Flag Protection Act unconstitutional, and Justice William Brennan wrote, "Punishing

desecrations of the flag dilutes the very freedom that makes this emblem so revered, and worth revering." In other words, the American Constitution gives its citizens the right to voice its opinions, favorable or not—which is the essence of democracy.

But during the Vietnam protests, flag-burning was punished, and offenders were vilified. Any sign of dissent was considered unpatriotic, and thousands of "draft dodgers" were urged to get out of the country.

How, then, do citizens call attention to problems they see in government? Is it not a form of patriotism to question your country's involvement in a war that is killing thousands of young men? What is a citizen to do when no one will listen? Are some forms of protest more acceptable than others? How would *you* make yourself heard?

College campuses erupted when President Richard M. Nixon sent American troops into Cambodia. Having promised to shorten the war, clearly Nixon was extending it to another country. Students wore black armbands and stopped attending classes. Many colleges and universities closed early that year because so many students were boycotting classes. The protesting students came from all areas of academic achievement, including those graduating with honors, and all social classes: rich, poor, middle class. All males over eighteen stood to be drafted, and once school deferments were abolished, the war affected everyone equally.

Part of the students' protest was against the government decision to draft first those students at the bottom three quarters of their class. Since the professors were responsible for ranking students, their decisions meant eligibility for many students. If professors were to stop issuing letter grades, giving pass/fail instead, the government would not know which students were subject to early draft.

Protesting is a right of democracy. You are no less patriotic if you protest against that which you believe to be wrong. Thousands of people protested the Vietnam War.

It was a time of great turmoil and fear. The protesters voiced legitimate concerns, if not always in a legitimate manner. Remember, the students believed the United States was fighting a war that was not winnable. They believed that sending more men to die in combat was a waste of the nation's human resources. They could see that the economy could not long support a draining war. And they certainly did not want to be the ones sent to die. Some people objected to the war on moral grounds; others, on principle: Who was the United States to meddle in another country's affairs? Whatever their objections, protesters were not necessarily cowards.

With the campuses aflame, authorities were at a loss as to how to maintain order. At Kent State University, the governor of Ohio called in the National Guard to restore peace. During a demonstration on May 4, 1970, National Guard members shot and killed four students and wounded nine others. In a less publicized incident on May 14, police and state highway patrolmen fired automatic weapons into a dorm at Jackson State University in Mississippi, attempting to break up a protest. Two students were killed and nine wounded.

The Vietnam war ended and so did the protests. Had they served to shorten the war? Had they stirred the American conscience, causing people to look at what was happening to their young people? Were not the protesters acting out of love of country, and is that not the definition of patriotism?

Senator George Mitchell of Maine once said, ". . . In America, disagreement with the policies of the government is not evidence of a lack of patriotism. . . . Indeed, it's the very fact that we can openly disagree with the government without fear of reprisal that is the essence of our freedom, and will keep us free."

ANDREI SAKHAROV

In a totalitarian government, where every aspect of life is controlled and monitored by the government, dissidents are not tolerated any more than protesters. There is a degree of difference between the two terms: A protester is one who acts out his dissent, whereas a dissident may only record his.

Protesting is not tolerated by a totalitarian government, even when the protester is someone as influential as scientist Andrei Sakharov.

Andrei Sakharov was one of the most famous Soviet dissidents. Because he was a highly respected nuclear scientist (largely responsible for developing the Soviet hydrogen bomb), the Soviet Union at first tolerated his criticisms. What were Sakharov's objections? He wrote against the building of nuclear weapons and the arms race and he warned of the danger to the environment even of nuclear testing. He continued to speak out against Soviet repression of its people, and in 1970 he founded the Committee for Human Rights in the Soviet Union. Through the committee he advocated "freedom of the press, an end to secret trials, amnesty for all prisoners, prison reforms, and abolition of the death penalty."

In 1975 he was awarded the Nobel Peace Prize. But even Sakharov could go too far, and when he condemned the 1979 Soviet invasion of Afghanistan, he was banished from Moscow to the city of Gorki, where he was kept under watch. Worldwide protests arose, and in 1986 he was released.

Freedom-lovers everywhere applauded Andrei Sakharov for trying to change his government. He could have fled abroad, but he chose to remain in the Soviet Union and fight unfair practices from within.

GANDHI

Mohandas Gandhi learned about civil disobedience from Henry David Thoreau when Gandhi spent his young adult-hood in South Africa. The practice of apartheid (separation of the races) cast him in an inferior role to the ruling whites, despite his being a well-to-do lawyer. Because Gandhi sought to challenge the apartheid laws, he was often arrested and spent time in jail. Reading Thoreau, he learned the power of nonviolent protest.

Returning to his native India, Gandhi spent the next three decades "resisting" to secure his country's independence from England. He staged sit-ins, fasted, and encouraged strikes and boycotts of British goods in protest against British rule. At first the government ignored or ridiculed this unimposing Indian, but when they realized the power of his nonviolent non-compliance, they hastened to jail him. Imprisonment only made his power greater, and eventually England chose to bargain with him. By resisting, without violence, Gandhi won independence for India in 1947.

TIENANMEN SQUARE

In China, students calling for democracy and an end to govern-ment corruption took over Beijing's Tienanmen Square in April 1989. Music of the American sixties blared from their boom boxes, and the public seemed buoyed by the spirit of protest. The students' challenge to the Communist govern-

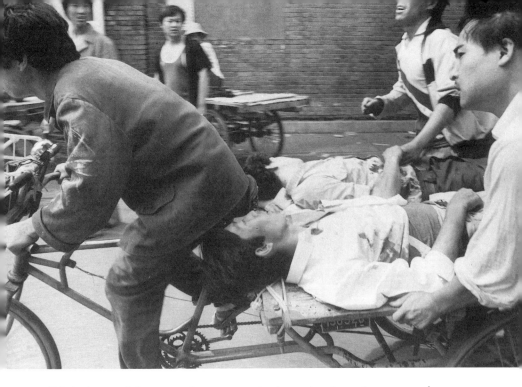

Rickshaw drivers take wounded protesters to a nearby hospital.

ment intrigued the rest of the world. Here were young men and women daring to speak out against a totalitarian regime. How would the government respond? Soviet President Mikhail Gorbachev was visiting Beijing that April, and the students remained unmolested in Tienanmen Square. As soon as he left, however, the troops moved in. The government declared martial law on May 19, but still the world thought the protest could be resolved peacefully. The students asked to meet with the Communist government; many thought it was possible. But the meeting never took place. Instead, on June 4 troops fired on the students. Western journalists and television crews were ordered away from the Square, but the world still learned that thousands of students had been killed. Within days the government authorized the army to shoot on the spot anyone accused of resisting arrest. Many protesters fled the country or sought immunity in foreign embassies. Most of the student leaders were killed. The Tienanmen Square rebellion was over.

Even as the twentieth century draws to a close, in some countries one can still risk his life in speaking out against injustice. That is the highest price a patriot pays in the cause of freedom. The lesson of all these protest movements is that speaking out can be just as patriotic a deed as singing the national anthem or fighting your country's wars.

PART IV
PATRIOTISM AND FREEDOM

CHAPTER 11

The Specter of Communism

At the conclusion of World War II, the United States and the Soviet Union emerged as the two world superpowers. Allies during much of the war, it was nonetheless an uneasy alliance. Josef Stalin, a ruthless dictator, ruled the Soviet Union. Under communism there was no freedom of speech, assembly, or religion. The United States suspected Stalin of planning to extend his boundaries and impose Communist rule on other countries.

In the United States, the wartime forties gave way to the prosperous fifties. Suburbs sprang up outside major cities, and a new way of life emerged. Women stayed home to tend their families; labor-saving appliances gave people more leisure time; television became the newest luxury. With a resurgence of conservatism and an emphasis on materialism, the idea of communism was frightening. No one wanted to lose the freedoms they enjoyed or give the government the fruits of their labors.

Joseph R. McCarthy, a United States Senator from Wisconsin, tapped into this Communist hysteria to make a name for himself, without evidence accusing various persons of Communist Party membership or sympathies. It is a sad

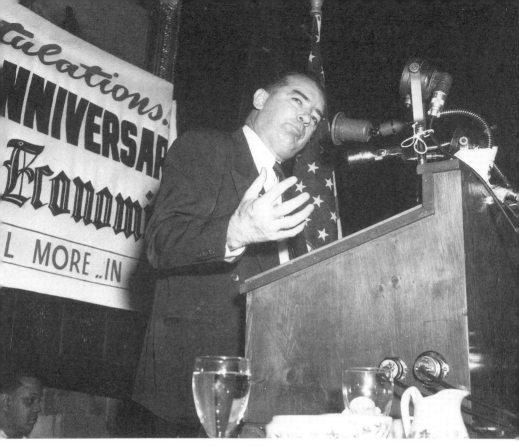

Senator Joseph R. McCarthy in 1954.

commentary on the times that no one initially challenged his allegations.

McCarthy first came to attention in 1950 when he charged that Communists had infiltrated the State Department. No evidence was ever adduced for his accusations; however, he continued his smear campaign, accusing more high-ranking public officials as well as ordinary citizens of subversive activities. His sway extended to Hollywood, where a "black list" of suspected Communists or Communist sympathizers was developed. Numerous prominent actors, directors, writers, and composers were accused and summarily fired or became unable to find work.

In 1953 McCarthy became chairman of a Senate sub-committee on investigations and gave full rein to his accusations. Ultimately, in 1954, he accused the Army of concealing espionage activities. In rebuttal, the Secretary of the Army charged that McCarthy's staff members had threatened Army officials, and a full-scale Senate investigation ensued. During the hearings, which were carried on television and widely publicized, McCarthy continued his wild accusations and became a controversial figure throughout the land. Although he was cleared of the specific charges against him, the Senate voted to condemn him for his methods. He retained his seat, however, and died in office in 1957.

How had America let McCarthy ruin so many people's lives? Fanatical in its fear of communism, the country reacted on emotion. Had facts been demanded first, it would have become clear that Senator McCarthy possessed very few. Whereas McCarthyism was initially associated with patriotism, it has ever since been connected with smear tactics.

When you begin taking away people's rights—even the right to hold Communist beliefs—you end up with less democracy. The Constitution gives us all the freedom to think as we want, to speak out, and to hold meetings. When you start curtailing rights that you disagree with, you create less freedom for all.

Joseph McCarthy was a dangerous man, for he preyed on what was then the country's greatest fear. For a while he got away with it—until people started to become afraid of *him*. Has the country changed since the fifties? Could a similar hysteria be created today? Has the country grown wiser?

CHAPTER 12

Nationalism and Independence

Nationalism need not be a dirty word, even though it has been associated with Hitler's regime and the Japanese Imperial Army. In many instances, nationalism, a love for one's country and a desire to set it above all others, has been responsible for the reemergence of small countries and ethnic groups. No better example exists than in Poland.

LECH WALESA

Poland is a country that has rarely been left alone by other countries. Greedy neighbors have always wanted its access to the sea. So, over the centuries, Poland has been swallowed up by countries to its east and west. During those periods of occupation, the Polish people remained faithful to their culture. It was considered patriotic to continue to speak Polish despite the usurper's influence and to attend the Catholic Church.

World War II officially began when Germany marched into Poland and partitioned the land with the U.S.S.R. Later, the Soviet Union occupied all of the country and installed the (Communist) Polish Committee of National Liberation. Although free elections had been promised, the Polish people were allowed to vote only for candidates selected by the Communist Party. Under communism, food prices soared and wages plummeted. The Party officials lived well; the poor suffered. In 1956 the people of Poznan rioted against conditions; the riots resulted in many deaths, but they signaled the beginning of the labor movement in Poland.

Lech Walesa, born in 1943, went to work in the Gdansk shipyards as a very young man and experienced firsthand the appalling working conditions. He believed the Polish people needed a labor union to protect their rights—but a union free of Communist Party influence. So he began organizing. He handed out pamphlets on street corners and encouraged workers to strike. Initially, Walesa was not trying to change the government; he was organizing a free labor union to ensure the people better working conditions, higher pay, and job stability.

Even though the government was ostensibly run by Polish officials, they owed allegiance to the Soviet Communist Party. If they failed to keep the workers in line, they would be blamed and replaced. Needless to say, the government took a dim view of Walesa and his activities. For a while the government alternately squelched the labor movement and ignored it. In 1980, however, as Lech Walesa's power and visibility increased, the government officially recognized Solidarity, the newly chosen name of the labor organization. Solidarity was an independent labor movement, and Walesa was at last granted the chance to organize the "common man."

As in most movements, Solidarity contained some radical elements who wanted more than economic reform and union representation. They blamed the government for the exorbitant food prices and the poor man's way of life. Unwilling to tolerate open dissent, Poland declared martial law in 1981 and charged Walesa and other Solidarity leaders with fomenting rebellion. Walesa was imprisoned, and Solidarity went underground. By this time, Solidarity had impressed countries around the world by its stand against communism, and it survived, in part because of quiet support from the United States and from Pope John Paul II, who is Polish. Solidarity

ZĄDAMY ZALEGALIZ...
NSZZ - SolidaRNosc
NIE ODDAMY SIĘ

was outlawed in 1982 in an attempt to break its hold on the people, but the movement did not die. Released from prison in 1982, Walesa was awarded the Nobel Peace Prize in 1983.

The Polish people were still hungry. Food prices remained high, people worked long hours for low pay. Members of Solidarity began to agree that the government had to go: Communism was hurting the economy and was antithetical to Roman Catholicism. After Mikhail Gorbachev came to power in the Soviet Union in 1988, Prime Minister Vojciech Jarulzelski permitted some reforms. He freed the press to print accurate stories about the economic situation, and he released political prisoners. In 1989 he went even further: He legalized Solidarity once again. By then, the Berlin Wall had been torn down, anti-Communist revolts were sweeping Eastern Europe, and the Soviet Union was loosening its grip on countries. Lech Walesa was elected president of Solidarity, and Poland formed the first non-Communist government in a Soviet-bloc country. Poland was not entirely free, however, until the people voted in the first free election for president in 1990. Lech Walesa was chosen and was sworn in as president on December 22, 1990.

That Solidarity was able to bring down the government of Poland demonstrates several things. First, that being a patriot requires great commitment and carries a heavy cost. When totally dedicated to a cause, one risks not only his physical life, but his life with his family. Cast into the limelight and occasionally thrown into prison, Lech Walesa had little time or energy to devote to his sizable family. His wife carried that burden alone. Second, Solidarity showed that patriotic movements can survive being outlawed, particularly if they can find outside support. In Poland's case, the United States provided money, technical services, and hope; the Vatican provided information and faith. Nonetheless, Poland owes its freedom to the tenacity and bravery of the outspoken Lech Walesa.

Lech Walesa, creator and leader of the Polish labor union Solidarity and current president of Poland.

THE SOVIET COUP

The world has undergone many changes undreamed of ten or even five years ago. In August 1991, while Soviet President Gorbachev was on vacation, the Red Army instigated a coup. Hardliners had worried that communism was dying under Gorbachev's regime. So, while Gorbachev was at his vacation home Soviet tanks moved into Moscow, pointing their guns at the White House, headquarters of Boris Yeltsin, president of the Russian Republic. Gorbachev and his family were held under house arrest.

The coup might have succeeded had it not been for that one man in the White House. Boris Yeltsin stepped outside to confront the troops (and the guns pointed his way). The troops had orders to kill Yeltsin, but they held their fire. Shocking everyone, Yeltsin climbed onto one of the tanks and shook hands with a soldier. Having supported the troops in the past, he viewed them as allies, and they did not let him down. Defying orders, they turned their guns around to defend the White House from further attack. The Russian people, realizing their victory, climbed onto the tanks as well, as the media scrambled to record the historic moment when the Soviet Union began to collapse.

Gorbachev, who had returned to power after the short-lived coup, resigned as head of the Soviet Union in December. Yeltsin, as president of the largest republic in the Soviet Union, assumed primary leadership. But once communism had lost its power, the republics began to clamor for independence. They had never lost their pride or sense of history. Hungary, East Germany, and Czechoslovakia had already gained freedom from Soviet rule, and other countries now sought the same freedoms. Latvia, Estonia, and Lithuania were the first to gain recognition as independent states. Ukraine, Moldova,

One of the many soldiers who defied orders and responded to Boris Yeltsin's resistance against the military coup. The old Russian flag flies from his tank.

Georgia, and Armenia followed. The Soviet Union continued to disintegrate as the nationalities fought for separate status.

Nationalism caused the drive for independence in the first place, but now nationalism threatens to tear apart some countries that cannot blend their ethnic groups into one nation. Czechoslovakia has separated into two countries, the Czech republic and Slovakia.

Ethnic factions have torn Yugoslavia into several parts: Bosnia and Herzegovina, Serbia, Croatia, and Montenegro. The Serbians in Bosnia and Herzegovina have engaged in a violent struggle to drive out almost one million Muslims and Croats. The result has been civil war, complete with detention camps and atrocities, that has confounded the United States and other countries in efforts to provide relief. Does "ethnic cleansing" have anything to do with patriotism?

Other countries around the world have fought for independence and won. Nationalism gave the people the desire to keep struggling in the face of great odds. Nationalism has also spurred countries to try to take over smaller, weaker ones, and in some cases to attack its own divergent populations. Love of country and intolerance for others sometimes combine in nationalism. Consider what happens when nationalism and patriotism go too far afield.

PART V

CAN PATRIOTISM GO TOO FAR?

CHAPTER 13

Hitler and the Nazi Party

As you begin this chapter, bear in mind that love of power does not equal love of country. Adolf Hitler was fanatically devoted to his country, but he was even more obsessed with power and exterminating those he didn't like or understand. You who are almost two generations removed from World War II may think that someone like Hitler could never emerge again. This then should be understood: Under the guise of patriotism, one man convinced all of Germany that it was patriotic to murder six million people. He began inauspiciously enough as a student.

Adolf Hitler was a poor student with an above average facility for drawing. However, he was unable to impress anyone enough to gain entrance to art school. Unwilling to believe that he lacked talent, he blamed the Jews, who were an extremely self-supportive and therefore prosperous community, and thus began his hatred for Jews.

After a number of aimless years, Hitler volunteered for the German army when World War I broke out; he was wounded and gassed, and served with some distinction. His experience deepened his fondness for authoritarianism and the glory of war. Violently opposed to the peace settlement, Hitler joined the German Workers' Party and devoted himself to it. Renamed the Nationalsozialistische Deutsche Arbeiterpartei (shortened to "Nazi"), the party rose rapidly and Hitler with it. His singlemindedness and his power as a speaker brought him to high office within the party and eventually to the chancellorship of Germany. In 1934, when the president died, Hitler had so consolidated his power that he was able to force the merging of the chancellorship and the presidency, and he assumed total control of Germany.

Most people failed to realize the extent of Hitler's ambition. They approved his efforts to restore German pride, which had suffered greatly in defeat. They did not recognize that his goal was annihilation of those he despised and ultimate world domination.

How could Hitler fool so many people? For one thing, he lied. He believed that the bigger the lie, the more believable it became. Also, he had an uncanny gift for feeling out the people and then using their own emotions to sway their thinking. People gave in to emotion around Hitler; they didn't listen to reason. They also believed that Hitler was a patriot; after all, he extolled the virtues of Germany and wanted to make it great again. What they did not know was at what expense.

Once in power, Hitler passed an act that permitted him to suspend the constitution and change or enact any law he deemed necessary. Now that Hitler *was* the law, his word required obedience without question. He then started to implement his plan to make Germany great again. He believed the Germans were a superior race. To keep the race pure, he first had to dispose of millions of people he judged to be inferior. Overrunning Poland, he began the systematic torture and murder of the Polish people. Then he turned his attention to the Gypsies, the Jews, homosexuals, and political dissidents.

Why did reasonable people not object to Hitler's methods? For one thing, reasonable people were not part of his inner

Hitler's Nazi Youth march before him at a parade in Nuremberg in 1936.

circle. For obvious reasons, he attracted to him people of similar beliefs and prejudices. Hermann Göring, German field marshal, once proclaimed, "I have no conscience." Hitler and his men preferred cruelty to mere violence, to break people's will to resist.

The Germans had to understand that the prosperity of the Jews was the reason for Germany's downfall, and the Jews must be punished, if not destroyed. Hitler devised an elaborate plan to indoctrinate the people with his thinking. He started with the children. Boys joined Youth for Boys, and girls joined the League of German Maidens. One did not join freely, as you would the Boy Scouts or Girl Scouts. Membership was mandatory; failure to join resulted in a quick trip to the orphanage. In these groups, the children learned their ultimate purpose in Hitler's society. Boys would become soldiers who would willingly die for Hitler. Girls would become good mothers to a new generation of Germans.

Hitler explicitly stated the new rules of his totalitarian regime. He controlled every aspect of the people's lives. He had spies to inform on nonconformists. Children were taught to turn in their parents if the parents disparaged the regime. Books were banned; freedom of the press no longer existed. Women were only good for supplying malleable recruits: children. To remain childless was therefore unpatriotic.

Hitler molded the youth by stamping out all sentiment in children. He once remarked, "I want a violent, arrogant, fearless, cruel youth who must be able to suffer pain." His soldiers helped to create that youth. Hitler sought to take the place of these children's parents. He became their protector, just as they ultimately would become his protectors when they fought for the Fatherland. Hitler then made them believe that "the strong have the right to destroy the weak." He cultivated in them contempt for the "inferior." By the time these youths were old enough for war, they showed fanatic devotion to Hitler and would rather die than fail in a mission for him. These, then, were the men who could send six million people to their deaths.

Hitler demonstrated his contempt for humanity in his manner of waging war. He ordered destruction of whole cities. Ninety percent of Warsaw, for example, lay in ruins after his army marched through. Hitler showed no compassion for anyone, including old people, women, and children. People were expendable if they did not serve his purpose. He looted the cities, took the country's children, and made them into slaves. When these children were no longer useful, they were either killed or left to die.

Although many Germans turned a blind eye to Hitler's atrocities, not everyone supported him. Hans and Sophie Scholl formed a resistance movement called The White Rose. They distributed pamphlets on street corners, letting the German people know the truth of what was happening elsewhere in the world. They knew they would be killed if they were caught, but it was more important to try to stop Hitler. Before they were put to death, they said, "To love one's country . . . means opposing it when it is wrong."

The world had to coin a word to describe Hitler's greatest atrocity: genocide, extermination of a racial, political, or national group. By the end of World War II in 1945, Hitler had systematically murdered six million people, most of whom were Jewish. Many people today question how this mass extermination, called the Holocaust, could have happened. Unfortunately, it was all too easy. In the beginning, Hitler merely "identified" the Jews and singled them out for contempt. Then, he stripped them of their citizenship and rights. The harassment of the Jews, coupled with the indoctrination of prejudice in German youth, was so gradual that most people accepted it as logical. Finally, Hitler sent the Jews to concentration camps for extermination. He created six camps for this purpose: Chelmno, Belzek, Sobibor, Treblinka, Majdanek, and the largest, Auschwitz.

Those persecuted people who had not managed to escape Germany and other occupied countries were jammed standing into boxcars like cattle to the slaughterhouse and delivered to the death camps. Most met immediate death in the gas chambers. The hardier ones were made to work until they died or lost their usefulness; some were used as human guinea pigs for Dr. Joseph Mengele's inhuman medical experiments. All were tattooed with numbers, starved, tortured, and stripped of their possessions (including clothes) and dignity. Most were separated from their loved ones. As horrendous as the details are, it is important to know what happened at these death camps to be certain that it never happens again. Almost an entire people was destroyed out of devotion to one man who believed that the greatness of his country rested on the murder of others.

The atrocities perpetrated in the camps raise the question: Who were those men who would blindly follow orders to kill innocent people?

Many of the camp guards were the very ones who claimed to be without conscience—men who would be attracted to Hitler's program in the first place. All had been steeped in his racist ideology; they believed they were the superior race and that they were meant to destroy the weak. They did not view Jews as victims or even as human. You do not feel guilty if you do not recognize wrong. If you cannot empathize with your victim, you cannot feel remorse. And finally, for those men, patriotism meant doing Hitler's bidding.

Adolf Hitler demanded total loyalty from his officers, and until the last year of war received it. One general, Friedrich von Paulus, defied Hitler's direct order not to advance in Russia because he realized he would be sentencing his own soldiers to death. Another general, Dietrich von Choltitz, defied a direct order from Hitler even though his defiance could have caused the death of his family. Toward the end of the war, Hitler had passed a law permitting him to execute the family of any officer who refused a direct order. He resorted to such ruthless tactics when his military men began to question the logic—and ethics—of his actions. In 1944, as Allied forces were marching toward German-occupied Paris, Hitler ordered General von Choltitz to destroy the city. He had already destroyed most of Warsaw and had shown that he was perfectly willing to destroy London during the Battle for Britain. Now he wanted to obliterate Paris so that nothing would be left for the Allies to liberate.

Von Choltitz had every opportunity to accomplish the razing of Paris. In the end, however, he could not bring himself to comply with such an inhuman command. As history has shown, Paris survived, in no small part because one German general chose to defy Hitler.

Adolf Hitler committed suicide in 1945 as Russian troops

converged on Berlin. By then he knew he had lost his war, and most people rejoiced that he was finally gone. Nevertheless, some men and women today admire and seek to emulate Hitler. In 1993 the German government was faced with an upsurge of violence by young neo-Nazis. Prejudice and intolerance still exist, and when they combine with patriotic fervor, anything can happen . . . again.

CHAPTER 14

Japanese Internment in World War II

When Japan attacked Pearl Harbor on December 7, 1941, the United States was justifiably enraged. And un-forgiving. Men eligible and ineligible for battle volunteered for service to avenge the Americans gunned down by the Japanese. Patriotic fervor sent thousands off to war for their country.

But in their fervor, patriotic Americans acted irrationally. Fearing that the Japanese had spies in the United States and were about to launch an attack on the West Coast, these Americans decided to take counteraction. At the time of World War II, 127,000 Japanese Americans lived in the United States. Two thirds of them were native-born American citizens, but that did not make them any less suspect. In the name of patriotism, Americans destroyed businesses, burned homes, and generally harassed the Japanese Americans. Banks refused to cash their checks; insurance companies canceled their policies. Many Japanese Americans were forced to sell their homes and businesses; few received support from their fellow Americans.

Under public pressure, President Franklin Delano Roosevelt signed Executive Order 9066, which authorized the Secretary of War to declare certain areas of the United States "danger zones" and to evacuate people from those zones to housing elsewhere. The order sounded innocuous enough, but it was clearly aimed at the Japanese Americans, who mostly lived in California, Oregon, and Washington. It was an attempt to rationalize the incarceration of thousands of citizens. In the spring and summer of 1942, the government moved 112,000 Japanese Americans to special internment camps.

Most of them willingly left their jobs and their homes and moved to the camps, which were built in ten isolated, barren sites in the interior. Their acceptance of such injustice reflects their desire to demonstrate their loyalty to their country. Some of the houses were one-room (20 by 25 feet) wooden barracks covered with tarpaper. Two- and three-generation families were expected to exist in these shacks.

Why had Americans been so quick to see the enemy in the Japanese Americans? Was it patriotic to turn on these people? History suggests that many Americans had envied the Japanese Americans' ability to build thriving businesses. Some envied their close-knit families and their reverence for the old, especially if they could not duplicate that sense of loyalty in their own families. Thus, some historians believe that jealousy drove them to react so strongly. They were the ones who bought out the displaced Japanese Americans. Or did Americans overreact because they needed to punish someone for Pearl Harbor and these people were such convenient targets?

Many Americans believed that since the Japanese had unscrupulously bombed Pearl Harbor without any declaration of war, they might likewise use spies based in America to perpetrate an attack on the mainland. In the end, reason and prudence gave way to panic.

So in the name of patriotism, 112,000 Americans were imprisoned for the duration of World War II. Not a single Japanese American was ever convicted of espionage against the United States. Even more ironic, those same "potential spies" remained subject to the draft. Some 8,000 Japanese American men served in the U.S. forces, many with distinction. Japanese women in the internment camps wove camouflage netting for the soldiers.

Who were the patriots in this scenario, the Americans who imprisoned their fellow citizens, or the Japanese Americans who continued to support a government that had imprisoned them?

A Japanese-American family tagged with shipping labels await transportation to an internment camp.

CHAPTER 15

The Ku Klux Klan—Lessons of Hate

After the American Civil War, Northern businessmen swooped down on the South, ostensibly to aid in its rebuilding. Reconstruction was one of the darkest periods in Southern history, as so-called Carpetbaggers and Scalawags tried to take control of local government. Southerners already had to adjust to a new way of life, rediscover their dignity, and find new jobs. They did not want Northerners telling them how to live as well.

Bored and dispirited, a group of Southern men decided to form a secret club for "merrymaking." It started as a joke. Masquerading in sheets, the men rode through the countryside, mostly to startle their own families. Other men sensed, however, that this club could serve another more serious purpose, and the Ku Klux Klan was born.

Robert E. Lee, the Confederate general, was approached to lead the Klan. General Lee endorsed the group, whose aim now was to frighten the Carpetbaggers and Scalawags out of the South, but he declined to participate. Instead, he recommended Nathan Bedford Forrest, another Confederate war hero, and thus Forrest became the first Grand Wizard of the Ku Klux Klan.

The Klan boasted a secret army of 100,000 men, and between 1867 and 1870 it waged a war for political control of the South. Wearing capes and hoods lent an air of mystery to the Klansmen and frightened their victims, who could never be certain just who their adversaries were. They terrorized blacks only to keep them from voting the way they believed the Northerners had programmed them. By 1870 the Klan had run the Carpetbaggers out of office. Forrest declared the objective met and disbanded the Ku Klux Klan.

But the KKK never disappeared completely. Some members were reluctant to give up their new-found power. While most of the secret army disbanded, some Klans remained active, focusing on a different enemy. Over the years they faded into the background, only to be revived when white supremacy seemed threatened. For some people, the power to terrorize others anonymously brought out the worst aspects of their nature. Under the guise of patriotism, hooded men could take to the countryside, safely giving vent to their racist ideology.

The year 1915 saw another revival of the Ku Klux Klan, mostly in Alabama and Georgia. By then, the targets had expanded to include blacks, Jews, Catholics, and immigrants. In a bid for respectability and to increase membership, promoters of the Klan tried to stir patriotic fervor. The program was billed as a return to "100 percent Americanism," but their brutal acts were fueled by hatred and bigotry.

Sometimes people try to justify unethical behavior by labeling it patriotic. Is a group really displaying love of country when it terrorizes a part of the population? What does it tell you when a supposedly patriotic group has no ideals and no positive programs? The Ku Klux Klan is based on negatives: getting rid of people to whom it objects.

Between 1925 and 1928, the Ku Klux Klan was at its height. Klansmen terrorized their victims by burning their homes, destroying their businesses, and—their favorite method of torture—flogging them. Just the sight of a cross afire on someone's front lawn was enough to drive the homeowner out of a community. The burning cross was just the beginning of the harassment. Next came torture or death.

To what were Klansmen objecting? Usually any form of integration: interracial couples, black children in white schools,

"uppity" blacks, and Jewish or Catholic businessmen in previously all-Protestant communities. The Klan appealed to fanatics, people who wanted to oust or destroy anyone not white and Protestant. Because of its unethical and illegal activities, the Klan has risen and fallen in prominence through the years. In 1964, Mississippi saw the rise of the most vicious Klan group, bent on driving out the civil rights workers. The White Knights of Mississippi were suspected of almost 800 acts of terrorism.

Racist groups such as the KKK often have political ambitions. David Duke, a past national director of the Knights of the KKK, ran for United States President in 1980, in the Louisiana Presidential primary in 1988, and for Governor in 1990. People who knew Duke during his college days say he wore a Storm Trooper uniform complete with swastika around campus. People called him "the Nazi of LSU." Patriotic fervor coupled with racial intolerance is certainly reminiscent of the Nazis and the neo-Nazi parties of today.

The Ku Klux Klan is still thriving. Thom Robb, current Grand Wizard, estimates that 346 Klan groups are in existence. Hate crimes have escalated in recent years. Perhaps you've seen swastikas chalked on your school walls, or heard about racially driven shootings. The KKK relies on propaganda to reinvent history and foment political action.

Entire families join the Klan. People have joined when their neighborhoods became integrated. Belief that blacks (or Jews or Japanese) were gaining too great a foothold in "decent" white neighborhoods drove many people to consider illegal acts. They joined knowing that Klan members would understand how they felt and be willing to do something about it—more than likely terrorize their unwelcome neighbors into leaving. Ordinary Americans were drawn into the prejudices and terrorist practices of the Klan. Soon it did not seem so wrong to threaten one's nonwhite neighbors over the phone, or to fire guns through their windows. The end—protecting one's children from "inferior" races—justified the means.

Crosses burn at a 1991 Ku Klux Klan rally, the first in Missouri in twenty years.

Everyone should be concerned about racist groups that practice what they preach. The new Klan claims it no longer uses violence to achieve its goals; it is focused instead on winning political office to *legislate* its goals. People who have reason to know say that it indeed still relies on violence to achieve its goals, although they concede that it is also interested in holding office.

If you believe that a little bit of prejudice isn't such a terrible thing, consider some of Thom Robb's goals, as stated in a *Time* magazine interview:

- Posting soldiers at the Mexican border to stop the flow of illegal immigration.
- Quarantining all AIDS patients.
- Killing drug dealers.
- Stopping affirmative action.
- Eventually separating the races, perhaps by banishing blacks (with reparations) to Africa.

Thom Robb's new Klan sounds very much like a neo-Nazi organization. He still sells copies of *Mein Kampf*, Hitler's manifesto, and he asserts that the Holocaust is a hoax.

In general, the Ku Klux Klan appeals to alienated white youth, who probably see an opportunity to better themselves in a society promoting white supremacy. The bad news is that the country today has a large number of "alienated white youth." And although Robb has tried to polish the Klan's image (having members wear business suits), it is still a racist organization. Michael Riley commented in the *Time* article, "Whether the Klan wears a hood and a robe or a business suit, its message is unchanged."

Remember the type of person Hitler attracted to his regime. If patriotism is a virtue, by definition it has nothing to do with terrorism.

CHAPTER 16

Terrorism

Terrorism would not seem to be the forte of a patriot, but incredibly that is what many terrorists proclaim themselves to be. How is that possible? People sometimes go to extremes out of love of country. But should that include taking innocent people hostage? Should it include blowing up airliners to attract attention to one's cause? That is exactly what many Middle East terrorists have done in the name of patriotism.

The Ayatollah Ruhollah Khomeini came to power in Iran in February 1979. In the preceding years, the United States had supported Muhammad Reza Pahlavi, the Shah of Iran. The wealthy Shah had alienated many of his people, particularly the ayatollahs, the Islamic leaders, by allying himself with Western governments. The ayatollahs resented his introduction of Western ideas to Iran; they believed he was turning his back on Islam, which to them was more than a religion. Islam was a way of life. It interpreted the laws, dictated the transaction of business deals, and shaped behavior in the social and political realms.

As Iran, under the influence of the clergy, grew more hostile toward the West, particularly the United States, the

Shah saw his power waning. When the people rose up in revolution, the Shah fled his country. Within days, Khomeini returned from exile in France to glory in Iran.

Under Khomeini, the Iranians grew increasingly militant toward the United States. When Washington refused to turn over the ailing Shah to his people (who wanted him executed), the United States became the number one enemy of Iran. And that made every American citizen its enemy, as well. On November 4, 1979, Iranian students seized the American embassy in Teheran. As the world watched in horror, the students chanted death threats to the Americans. Khomeini refused to order release of the hostages, and it soon became apparent that he endorsed the seizure.

Despite their holding more than fifty Americans in captivity for more than a year, the students considered themselves patriots. They were acting out of love for Iran, whose image and religion they believed had been demeaned under the Shah's American-backed regime. What was the hostage taking intended to accomplish? It actually did accomplish two things: First, it brought attention to the students' frustration; second, it humbled the United States, which, despite its might, could do nothing to get its people back. It did not, however, achieve the return of the Shah, who died in Egypt the following year.

Some historians say that President Jimmy Carter lost his chance for a second term because of his inability to end the hostage situation in Iran. Not until January 1981 did the Iranians release the Americans.

To further the revolution, Iranians created the Hizbollah or Party of God, a terrorist organization. Most of the terrorists who seized Americans and other nationals in Lebanon were connected with the Hizbollah and proudly claimed responsibility for their acts. The taking of hostages in Lebanon served several purposes, the most important of which was to

Iranian students demonstrate at the American Embassy in Teheran, demanding that the Shah be returned to Iran to be executed.

frighten Americans out of the Middle East. Terrorists also used hostages to call attention to their country's demands, to trade for fellow terrorists imprisoned in other countries, and to extort information. The latter is why they tortured and eventually killed William Buckley of the CIA.

Not only did Khomeini condone the kidnapping of American citizens, he further shocked the world when he called for the execution of Salman Rushdie, who he said had maligned the prophet Muhammad in his fictional work *The Satanic Verses*. On February 14, 1989 (almost ten years from the day he gained power in Iran), Khomeini issued a decree, "The author of *The Satanic Verses*, which is against Islam, the Prophet and the Koran, and all those involved in its publication who were aware of its content, are sentenced to death. I call on zealous Muslims to promptly execute them on the spot they find them so that no one else will dare blaspheme Muslim sanctities."

Teheran offered $2.6 million to Rushdie's executioner, with an additional $1 million if the executioner were an Iranian. As recently as July 1992, zealous Muslims were caught plotting Rushdie's death in Great Britian.

Most people agree that Khomeini's decree *is* unethical. But what should a devout Muslim do, faced with the dilemma of honoring his faith by killing another human being? Does he owe such allegiance to his country (and faith)? And what does he owe his fellow man? Is it right to deprive someone of life for the sake of honor? Loyal Muslims are still struggling with that dilemma while the rest of the world debates the right of free speech. Can a person kill a man for what he writes?

Another question to consider: Is it patriotic to support one's country at the expense of another? When war has been declared, defending one's country (even killing the enemy) demonstrates patriotism. But what happens when there *is* no war, and the only motivation to harm innocent people is to draw attention to a cause? The Palestine Liberation Organization (PLO), formed in 1964, has engaged in terrorism to draw attention to its demand for a homeland. For years the Israelis and Palestinians have disputed the Israeli-occupied West Bank and Gaza Strip, seized in the Six-Day War in 1967. The PLO, under the leadership of Yasir Arafat, are actually a people without a country. They have been domiciled and supported in Iraq, Syria, and Lebanon, but because of their terrorist activities they are barred by most countries.

Radical members broke with the PLO to form the Palestine Liberation Front. In 1985 this group hijacked the luxury liner *Achille Lauro* in the open sea as it neared Port Said, Egypt. They boarded the ship and eventually murdered an American passenger, Leon Klinghoffer, throwing both him and his wheelchair into the sea. They were demanding release of fifty Palestinians held by Israel. The terrorists bungled their mission, but Libya granted them permission to put ashore, and they went free.

Are terrorists more interested in exerting power than showing love of country? What role should principles play in patriotism? Can unprincipled men and women be patriotic?

The self-proclaimed patriots of the Middle East believe they have the right to murder in the name of a greater cause. Seeing themselves as oppressed and exploited, they believe they have the right to rectify their situation by whatever means. To them, murder in the name of patriotism becomes honorable. Is that possible?

Why has terrorism become so widespread? For one thing, because it works. Terrorists sought to restrict American travel in the Middle East, and they certainly have achieved that in the past decade. Terrorists wanted to humiliate the United States, and having held Americans hostage at various times since 1979, they have demonstrated their power. Terrorist acts always capture the world's attention by the very nature of their aggression. And finally, terrorist acts usually gain concessions. Despite public avowals to the contrary, many people are willing to deal with terrorists—if only because they see no other choice.

When terrorists target airports and airplanes, their bombings affect many more innocent people. To blow up an airplane to assassinate a specific person means killing scores of men, women, and children. Is it ever excusable to kill innocent people?

Consider the Iranian airbus disaster in July, 1988. The American destroyer *Vincennes* mistook the commercial plane for a hostile fighter and shot it down over Iranian waters, with a loss of 240 lives. A series of errors, not the least of

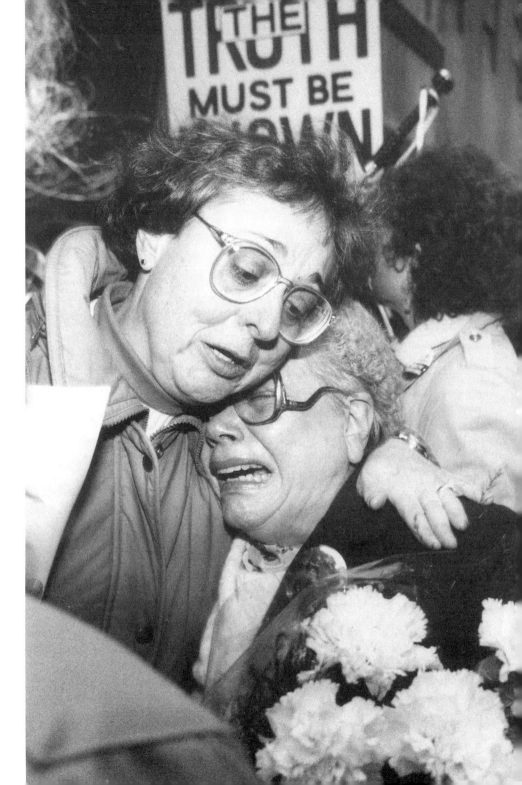

which was an eagerness to engage the enemy, led to the fatal mistake. The United States withheld information from the American public to make the attack appear less provocative than it had been, but the Iranians seemed to know exactly what had happened and promised retribution. When an American airliner (Pan Am Flight 103) blew up over Lockerbie, Scotland, in December, people immediately suspected the Iranians. The bombing cost 270 lives, including eleven on the ground. If, indeed, the first disaster inspired the second, had justice been served?

If we postulate that patriotism motivates terrorists to kidnap and hold hostages, what motivates the terrorists to mistreat those hostages? Men released by their Arab captors after years as hostages tell of being blindfolded most of the time, beaten and tortured, isolated from other prisoners, and kept in ignorance of world events. They were poorly fed and given little if any medical treatment. Love of country can in no way justify such callous disregard for human life.

Psychology offers an explanation for people's mistreatment of others. When people knowingly do evil, they often seek to rationalize their behavior by calling it something other than it is. Terrorists can feel noble despite their ignoble acts if they cloak them in righteous terms: love of country, patriotism. Some terrorists are simply fanatically devoted to a cause and lose sight of reason and fairness: to them, the end (however laudable) justifies the means (however heinous). But the term patriotic terrorist is surely an oxymoron. How can a lover of liberty, the traditional definition of patriot, be willing to deprive others of their liberty?

Mrs. John Bissett (right) mourns the loss of her son, Kenneth, during a demonstration against the terrorist bombing of Pan Am Flight 103.

PART VI

LOVE OF COUNTRY AND OTHER ISSUES

CHAPTER 17
Civil Rights

Now let's consider men and women who, out of love of country, sought to make their country and people better. These people, patriots in the true sense of the word, were not military heroes, but they were as strongly devoted to their cause as those who took up arms to defend it. Some gave their lives for their beliefs; most sacrificed their privacy and family life. Patriotism and commitment to high ideals always exact a price.

To understand the American civil rights movement of the 1960s, you must first examine its roots in slavery and the abolitionist movement. Slavery was not only inhumane but directly opposed to what America stood for. A country that had fought for independence and equal rights for all was actually denying those rights to some of its people. Of course, the abrogation of black people's rights was rationalized by considering slaves property, not human beings.

HARRIET BEECHER STOWE

Abolitionists faced an uphill struggle in gaining the country's support to end slavery. Southerners had grown up with slavery;

they accepted it as a way of life vital to their economy. Needing the slaves' free labor, and considering them subhuman anyway, many Southerners saw nothing wrong in what they were doing. Northerners were removed from the actuality of slavery and did not realize the extent of its inhumanities. For all they knew, the slaves were content with their lot, since they received free housing and food.

Harriet Beecher Stowe did for the slaves what journalists in Southeast Asia did for Vietnam. She opened the issue of slavery to the general public and exposed its ugliness to the world by writing *Uncle Tom's Cabin*, a book that followed the lives of several blacks in the South. While some say the book exaggerated the slave experience, it provided the necessary spur to public opinion. Published in 1852, the book sold 1.5 million copies worldwide and was especially revered in England. For many Americans, Harriet Beecher Stowe had personalized the slave experience in the characters of Uncle Tom and Eliza, and thus the abolitionist movement gained renewed momentum. Abraham Lincoln admired this woman who had dared write about an issue that so divided the nation. He jokingly referred to her as "that great lady who started" the Civil War.

FREDERICK DOUGLASS

Frederick Douglass, a famous abolitionist, was born into slavery in 1818. Exceptionally intelligent, he taught himself to read and write. It was against the law to educate a slave; realistically, it was feared that once a slave could read, he would realize his inferior status and would rebel or run away. Frederick Douglass did both. He ran away to New York at the age of twenty and then moved on to Massachusetts, where he was safer from being caught and returned to his master. In 1840, Douglass was asked to speak about his experiences at an abolitionist meeting. Like other charismatic men, Douglass

A daguerrotype of Frederick Douglass, circa 1850.

discovered his gift for moving people, and he continued to speak out against slavery. After writing *Narrative of the Life of Frederick Douglass*, he became so famous that he, and others, feared for his life. He could have stopped speaking; he could have been satisfied that at least **he** was free, but instead he felt compelled to fight against slavery until all blacks were free. To keep out of the public eye, Douglass lived for two years in England, where sympathizers purchased his freedom from his old master. Legally free, he returned to the United States and founded *The North Star*, an abolitionist newspaper. He also housed people who were escaping to freedom in the North on the Underground Railroad.

Frederick Douglass loved his country and his people, but he knew slavery had to be destroyed, and he dedicated his life to that end. During the Civil War, he encouraged blacks to join the Union cause. All three of his sons enlisted. He visited Abraham Lincoln to ask for equal pay for black troops, for retribution when black prisoners were tortured and murdered by Confederate soldiers, and for medals for the blacks who displayed heroism during the war. Lincoln did promise higher pay and medals for bravery, but the country was not yet ready for integrated troops and equal pay. After the war, Douglass was the only black delegate at a national convention called to decide whether to give black men the vote. He was instrumental in passage of the 15th Amendment to the Constitution guaranteeing that right. With his people's freedom and right to vote secure, Douglass spent his later years lobbying for equal rights for women.

HARRIET TUBMAN

Harriet Tubman was another former slave who risked her life again and again to bring freedom to her people. After having made her way to the North in 1849 via the Underground

Demanding equal rights for blacks "by any means necessary," Malcolm X was a highly influential leader in the sixties.

Railroad, she immediately returned to the South to help other slaves escape. She was responsible for at least 300 escapes, and a reward of $40,000 was offered for her capture. However, that did not stop Harriet Tubman, who even volunteered to serve as a spy for Union troops behind Confederate lines during the Civil War.

MARTIN LUTHER KING, JR.

Many Americans thought the issue of black rights was over once slavery was abolished and the right to vote was won. Turmoil in the 1950s and '60s demonstrated otherwise. Rosa Parks, a tired black woman who refused to give up her seat on a bus to a white man, showed the world that blacks still did not have the same rights as whites. Restaurants had separate entrances, drinking fountains, and restroom facilities for blacks. Blacks attended all-black schools, which were usually poorly funded and consequently of inferior quality. Blacks were allowed to sit only at the back of buses, and then only if no white wanted the seat. Is it surprising that people rose up to protest these conditions?

Martin Luther King, Jr. revitalized the civil rights movement in the '60s. People listened to him and followed him for several reasons. First of all, he was right. Blacks were being treated unfairly and inhumanely. Second, King was a charismatic speaker whose words and tone could stir crowds. And last, King believed in nonviolence to achieve his goal of full equality for all people. It was not his intention to turn the streets into battlezones, although those who rejected his ideals did just that. King organized sit-ins at lunch counters that were not open to blacks. He called for marches and demonstrations, and he participated in them himself. When Rosa Parks was jailed for her refusal to give up her seat on the bus, King ordered a strike of all public transportation. Blacks stayed away from the buses and rode bicycles or walked to work, and the bus owners had to reevaluate their position; they could not continue to run without their riders, most of whom had been blacks. Integrating the buses was King's first victory.

Martin Luther King was a hero to many young Americans, especially those in the North who were not routinely exposed to overt injustice to blacks. Here was a man who believed so strongly in a cause that he risked his life every time he took part in a march. He defied the laws because he believed them to be unethical, and he gave up his privacy and family life because the needs of his people took so much of his time. King was jailed more than once and received death threats to himself and his family. Yet he pressed on with his commitment to bring about equality through nonviolence. A 1963 march on Washington drew 250,000 people to protest inequality. In 1964 King was awarded the Nobel Peace Prize.

But some people in the civil rights movement were frustrated with the slowness of change. Malcolm X was a key spokesman for a group that advocated violence in their demand for equal rights. The Black Muslims believed that only blacks could free themselves, and they rejected both Martin Luther King's nonviolence and his white support. Black Power arose in the mid-'60s to challenge white supremacy and King's peaceful approach to ending it. Ironically, both men met violent deaths. Malcolm X was assassinated in 1965; Martin Luther King, Jr., in 1968.

Ideas do not die simply because men do. The Civil Rights Act of 1964, passed during President Lyndon Johnson's administration, secured greater equality for blacks. Martin Luther King's dream—that all men would live in peace and harmony—has yet to be met. But subsequent amendments to the act have further solidified black rights, and the world is a better place for his having worked toward that goal.

NELSON MANDELA

The United States had slavery and segregation; South Africa has apartheid. We saw in Chapter 3 that the Dutch, and then the British, took over South Africa, driving the native Africans back from the coast into the bush. The white minority seized power and passed laws to suppress the Africans and Indians. The fact that a small minority could so effectively overpower the majority of the population is astonishing. Laws were passed forcing blacks to live in squalid townships outside the cities. Blacks could enter the cities only to work, and even then they were required to carry passes. They could not enter "whites only" establishments, and more significant, they could not vote to change the laws that discriminated against them.

In 1912 Africans formed the African National Congress (ANC) to work for black rights. Nelson Mandela grew up under apartheid and knew it was wrong. Out of love for his country and his people, he sought to end apartheid and joined the ANC to work for that cause. Mandela was influenced by Mohandas Gandhi, who had lived in South Africa in the early 1900s. Gandhi practiced nonviolence in his struggle to end apartheid, and Mandela adopted nonviolence as well. He saw that violence in pursuit of their goals, they risked bringing dishonor to their cause.

Nelson Mandela was dedicated to his people and to bringing about an end to apartheid. Because of Mandela's dedication and effectiveness, the South African government saw him as a threat and "banned" him. That meant that he was not allowed to speak to crowds of people or attend any assembly, and that others were forbidden to speak to him. When banning failed to stop him, Mandela was jailed numerous times, but he continued to speak out for black rights. He refused to carry a pass because "as a citizen, as a black man, and as a person of conscience he had found himself unable to obey laws that were unjust, immoral, and intolerable because they were based on racial discrimination." Mandela's continued defiance inspired other blacks, so the government was finally moved to drastic action. Other highly visible men in the ANC had left South Africa to seek support for the cause. Mandela had left Africa once to study resistance methods in other countries, but he never intended to live outside of South Africa. In 1963 he was sentenced to life imprisonment on charges of plotting to overthrow the government.

Nelson Mandela has fought for most of his life for a free and democratic society in the Republic of South Africa.

Mandela had worked long and hard for equal rights, and finally, in frustration, he modified his nonviolent principles to permit destruction of property as a way of calling attention to his cause. His work now included violence, but he never countenanced injury to people.

Nelson Mandela's goal was a free and democratic society for all Africans: "It is an ideal which I hope to live for and to achieve. But if needs be, it is an ideal for which I am prepared to die."

Just as Gandhi's stature rose when he was imprisoned, so did Nelson Mandela's. The world demanded his release, and many countries joined to pressure South Africa into ending apartheid. In 1990, after twenty-eight years, President F.W. de Klerk freed Mandela from prison and lifted the ban that had been placed on the ANC. Mandela left prison a man of seventy-two but still fully capable of leading the ANC. In 1992 the people of South Africa voted to dismantle the laws supporting apartheid. Ironically, black Africans had no say in that vote. Much remained to be done, but the world at last had reason to hope that equal rights would come to South Africa.

The men and women in this chapter represent only a few of the people who have committed themselves to changing their country for the better. Most did not advocate violence in their pursuit of a better world, although they were often subjected to violence themselves. Without their efforts, we would live in a much harsher environment. As you consider the real patriots of the world, remember those who fought for your rights without ever firing a gun.

CHAPTER 18

Environmental Issues

What does it mean when a person says he loves his country? Is he (or she) talking about the land or the people? In this chapter, we examine those who consider the planet earth their country and what they are doing to protect it.

Many problems plague the earth today. When man invented the automobile—and other gas-guzzling modes of transportation—he did not know that he was hastening the earth's pollution. Huge factories give off smoke and gases that pollute the air we breathe and then descend to contaminate the soil and the lakes. Sulfur oxides are given off by fossil fuels such as coal. These oxides, released into the atmosphere, mix with fog and dust to cause corrosive smog and acid rain.

Because of acid rain, forests, animals, and crops are dying, and lakes and soils are turned acidic. Everything is related: Crops and forests are dependent on fertile soil; animals are dependent on clean water and healthy forests. When part of the system dies, the rest of the cycle suffers.

Environmentalists have warned for years that we were polluting the earth and might end up destroying the protective ozone layer that surrounds the earth, blocking the sun's

Canadian Colleen McCrory was awarded the Goldman Environmental Prize in 1992 for her work to protect British Columbia's largest remaining temperate rain forest.

harmful rays. Today, just as predicted, scientists are reporting holes in the ozone layer.

Activists are sometimes at a loss where to place the blame. Pollution in one country has direct impact on the forests and lakes of other countries. What is to be done when one's own country suffers because of the actions of one's neighbors? That is what happened in Sweden, where 82 percent of the acid rain is the result of foreign pollution—sulfurous oxides released from factories to the south and east. Sweden depends on timber for manufacturing; when the forests die, the soil erodes, and the pollutants in the soil run off into the lakes. Most plants and fish cannot survive in lakes that are too acidic.

Canada rightly blames the United States for polluting the rivers and lakes along the border. Northeastern factories spew gases into the air that blow across the border to Canada. Industries in the United States and Mexico alternately pollute each other's environment depending on which way the wind is blowing.

Environmentalists have reason to be alarmed when the earth's natural resources are dying of pollution. One of the ways they seek change is by persuading other countries to reduce emissions of harmful oxides in their factories as well as their vehicles. The Earth Summit in 1992 was the first time much of the world met to discuss cooperative action to protect the earth's natural resources. Although many countries disagreed on solutions, most realized the extent of the problems. Environmentalists had at least made the world aware.

People who fight to preserve the natural environment encounter the same difficulties as other patriots devoted to a cause. They risk their privacy and, on occasion, their lives. Colleen McCrory of Canada has spent years protesting the clear-cutting of forests in British Columbia. She worries that the public will not realize what they've lost until the forests are gone, the animal habitats destroyed, and the soil eroded. She founded the Future Forests Alliance, which calls for setting aside 12 percent of Canada's land as wilderness. Because of her crusading efforts, lumbermen and others dependent on the lumber industry put her out of business. Children taunted her own young children. Nonetheless she has persisted, as the rest of the world's concern catches up with hers.

Ecoterrorists represent a radical movement among environmentalists. They are far more aggressive in their efforts to protect the environment. Among them, Greenpeace adopts militant tactics in the knowledge that anything less has little or no deterrent effect. Greenpeace monitors the world for destruction of endangered species and actually invades fishing waters to protect fish and mammals. In the summer of 1992 Greenpeace activists took to the waters again to intervene

A Saudi Arabian information officer examines the oil-coated body of a cormorant. Saddam Hussein's order to dump 500 million gallons of oil into the Persian Gulf resulted in a slick forty times larger than the Exxon Valdez disaster and is expected to devastate the Gulf's wildlife for years to come.

in Norway's whale hunt. Norwegians had claimed that 86,000 minke whales lived in the North Atlantic, a sufficient number to warrant resumption of hunting. Greenpeace activists denied the claim and began monitoring the whalers' efforts. In July they used a dinghy to position themselves between the whalers and the whales. Unable to harpoon whales without possibly hitting the activists, the Norwegians called off the hunt.

Ecoterrorists use a variety of means including sabotage to deter others from harming the environment. Most stop short of hurting people, but not property. Given the seriousness of the problem, do you think that terrorists are "right" in employing such drastic means? Are prosecutors "right" to try them for their acts? Is punishment of ecoterrorists with fines or jail terms a fair price to pay to save the environment?

Much of the world's pollution has occurred by accident or through ignorance. Educating the public and passing legislation to force compliance will help to remedy that. But how should people be held accountable when they purposely damage the environment? During the Gulf War in 1991, Saddam Hussein ordered 500 million gallons of oil dumped into the Persian Gulf. The oil threatened not only the area wildlife, but other countries' water supplies as well (which may have been Hussein's intent). As the Iraqis fled Kuwait in the final days of the war, they blew up 640 oil wells, which precipitated an ecological disaster. Billowing smoke filled the atmosphere, blocking the sun and making it hard to breathe. Although several nations flew in teams to put out the fires and cap the wells, it was not until November 1991 that the last fire was extinguished.

Saddam Hussein unleashed chemical weapons on his own people as well as the Iranians during the Iran/Iraq war. Besides killing people, chemical weapons also destroy the environment, making the land useless for any purpose. Should one person be allowed to destroy the earth? If not, what should the world do about it? Demanding reparations from Iraq has made little impression on Hussein.

Ordinary people (those who take steps to conserve and protect their environment) are the heroes of this chapter. Trash is piling up all around the world; nuclear energy plants are looking for states and countries willing to accept their waste; the rain forests are being cut down; animals are losing their habitats and dying, and acid rain is rendering the lakes and soil useless. The men, women, and children who take this issue seriously and want to leave a better world to their own children are finding ways to conserve, recycle, and educate others. Being patriotic—loving the earth—does not always require monumental effort. The person who persuades a community to start a recycling program is just as much a hero as the one who joins Greenpeace.

CHAPTER 19

Women's Rights

How does a woman feel good about her country when she does not even have a say in its government? Hard as it is to imagine, women in most countries did not have the right to vote until well into the twentieth century. Women had to fight to win the right to own property, to gain custody of their children in a divorce settlement, and to vote. Although women had backed their countries and their men in times of war, they were not considered intelligent enough or stable enough to be allowed to vote. Beginning in the nineteenth century, many women put their lives on hold to fight for equal rights.

Woman suffrage was first achieved on the national level in 1893 in New Zealand, followed by Australia in 1902. American, British, and Canadian women did not win the same rights until the end of World War I. Most European countries granted suffrage around the same time, but Spain, France, and Italy did not follow until World War II, and Switzerland held out until 1971. Women in many Latin American countries received suffrage during the mid-1940s, whereas neither men nor women in African countries such as Uganda and Nigeria could not vote until the late 1950s and early '60s.

Two countries notable for women's struggle to achieve

equal rights are Great Britain and the United States. In Britain, the battle began when the philosopher John Stuart Mill offered a petition to Parliament calling for the inclusion of woman suffrage in the Reform Bill of 1867. When it was denied, Lydia Becker, who founded the first woman suffrage committee, took the issue to the public. Several committees quickly formed and united in 1897 as the National Union of Women's Suffrage Societies, with Millicent Garret Fawcett as president. Their goal was to overcome the traditional prejudices that suppressed women and denied them equal rights. Eventually frustrated by political impasse, some women resorted to militance. Emmeline Pankhurst, assisted by her daughters, Christabel and Sylvia, founded the Women's Social and Political Union in 1903. Known as "suffragettes," these women and their followers heckled politicians, fomented riots, and practiced civil disobedience until the beginning of World War I, when they suspended their own battle to support their country's war effort. In February 1918, women over the age of thirty received the right to vote, and in 1928, men's and women's suffrage rights became equal.

The women's rights movement in the United States began with the antislavery movement. As people began to question the black person's status (or lack of one), women came to realize that they lacked status as well. Married women had no rights to their property or their own children and could not vote to change the laws that discriminated against them.

The first American suffragists were Elizabeth Cady Stanton, the philosopher of the women's movement; Lucy Stone, its most brilliant orator; and Susan B. Anthony, its organizer. At first the goals were to gain for women: (1) control of their own property; (2) education; and (3) child custody, if they wanted it.

Working as a team, the women spoke at meetings, lobbied Senators and Representatives, and handed out pamphlets. Their efforts bore fruit, as in 1860 New York State passed a bill giving women the right to sue in court and to collect their own wages. Seemingly a small gain, it was nonetheless their first victory. With the coming of the Civil War, the women devoted their energies to fighting slavery. In 1867 they reorganized into the Equal Rights Association and fought to win the vote for black men as well as for women. Later this group became the National Women Suffrage Association. With the passage of the 14th and 15th Amendments to the United States Constitution, America finally conceded full rights of citizenship to black men.

Susan B. Anthony registered that year and tried to vote, but was arrested. A court declared her guilty of breaking the law by trying to vote, but public outcry brought about her release. Since Lucy Stone was busy with her own family, Susan B. Anthony took her place, lecturing around the country and lobbying legislators for a federal suffrage amendment. While the women's group splintered over methodology, Susan B. Anthony remained steadfastly dedicated to winning the right to vote. She served as president of the National American Association (the merger of the rival groups) until 1900.

As America entered World War I, the suffragists called President Woodrow Wilson two-faced for leading the country to war for "democracy" when American women couldn't even vote. By the end of the war, in 1920, the suffragists had prevailed upon Congress to adopt an amendment giving women the right to vote. But the struggle went on as the suffragists worked to persuade state legislatures to ratify the amendment. Because these women fought so hard, often sacrificing their personal lives and marriages, American women today can exercise the right to vote.

Winning the vote did not end women's dissatisfaction with the status quo in America. The feminist Betty Friedan in 1966 founded the National Organization for Women to help educate both men and women, and to fight to change the inequities still existing between the sexes. The 1970s saw a resurgence in the women's movement. This time, women were fighting for equal pay for equal work. Women in general were paid less than men for doing the same job. Women were also discriminated against in hiring; employers apparently believed one of two things: that women did not need jobs as much as men because they were not the breadwinners, or that women were not reliable employees because of their reproductive cycle.

Women sometimes fought aggressively for their rights.

Tradition has labeled assertiveness and tenacity as "male" traits; consequently, women who displayed those qualities were ridiculed as "masculine" and "unladylike." Aggressive men were "macho"; aggressive women were "bitches." Nonetheless, women continued to demand their rights. When growing numbers of women entered the professions traditionally reserved for men, many people assumed that the women's movement was over, its objectives met. Others claimed that it had failed its members because women could not handle equality, and they cited as evidence women's complaints about the difficulties of combining careers and motherhood.

The women's movement has not died, however. In 1991 a woman law professor brought to public attention the issue of sexual harassment in the workplace. The United States Senate had been holding hearings on the nomination of Clarence Thomas to be an associate justice of the Supreme Court. When the media received a tip that Clarence Thomas had been accused of sexual harassment, the search was on for the full story. Anita Hill came forward and made the charges before the Judiciary Committee. Clarence Thomas denied them. Professor Hill alleged that ten years earlier when she had worked for Thomas at the Equal Employment Opportunity Commission, he had used sexually explicit language and taunted her with graphic details of his sexual exploits. Clarence Thomas denied the allegations. The Committee struggled to understand the issue of women's exploitation in the workplace, but it was obvious from their televised comments that most of the fourteen men could not understand why a woman as capable as Anita Hill would have tolerated such behavior without challenging it. If Anita Hill accomplished nothing else, she succeeded in raising the level of awareness of sexual harassment in the workplace, but at a cost to her privacy.

Professor Anita Hill became nationally known when she put the needs of women before her own needs by publicly accusing Supreme Court nominee Clarence Thomas of sexual harassment.

Professor Hill has stated that she came forward out of a sense of duty. Given that her integrity was impugned, it hardly seems logical to suggest that she sought personal gain. In an interview on "60 Minutes" she said, "I did what my conscience told me I had to do." In the Senate hearings and in subsequent interviews, Anita Hill demonstrated courage and dignity under pressure—patriotic qualities.

Whatever the facts of the matter, the highly publicized controversy revitalized the women's movement. Women, some for perhaps the first time, realized their political clout as they watched the Senate hearings on television, and they vowed to vote out of office candidates who were unsympathetic to women's rights.

The struggle for women's rights goes on, as women in other countries are still treated unfairly. The Gulf War in 1991 demonstrated some of the inequities that exist. Women in the U.S. forces received instruction in how to behave so as not to offend their Arab hosts. Middle Eastern women must dress to conceal their bodies; they are not allowed to drive cars or to be alone with men. Their educational opportunities are inferior to men's. However, those women, especially the Iraqis and the Kuwaitis, demonstrated their nerve and stamina when they fought to preserve their families and their integrity during the war. They were not the helpless women of popular imagination; in fact, when the war ended, some were reluctant to resume their old ways.

It is hard to feel good about your country or yourself when you do not have the rights accorded to others. Loving one's country sometimes requires encouraging radical change to improve it. No country is truly free until its people are all equally free.

CHAPTER 20

The Disenfranchised

The disenfranchised are those people who have no rights, or who do not know how to exercise the rights they do have: the homeless and immigrants. Who champions these people? And what do these people think of the countries in which they exist without rights?

THE HOMELESS

The homeless in America are not a new phenomenon. You find people living in boxes or sleeping in subways or on park benches in most major cities. The rural homeless often live in abandoned cars or makeshift tents. What do these people think of America, the land of opportunity? Somehow, the system has failed them. Do they know that their country gives billions of dollars in relief to foreign countries? And that food supplies go overseas to starving children when their own children are starving right here in America?

Is it "right" for the United States to send aid to foreign countries when its own people are suffering?

Feeding and housing the homeless has not been a priority

for most legislators in the past. Legislators are more inclined to respond to people with clout. Most of the homeless do not vote and do not have relationships with voting relatives. Consequently they can't exert much pressure on community leaders or members of Congress.

Do you wonder, then, why the homeless do not protest their situation themselves? Certainly, spokesmen have existed, but in general the homeless do not lobby their Senators and Representatives for a very good reason. Consider the other causes to which people have devoted themselves, working tirelessly toward a goal. The homeless are *already* tired. They have no homes, no security, and in most cases no assurance that they will eat a decent meal that day.

The psychologist Abraham Maslow devised a hierarchy of needs to explain how people are motivated. Picture this hierarchy as a ladder. At the bottom of the ladder are our most basic needs: the need for clean air, water, food, and clothes. According to Maslow, when a person has satisfied those basic needs, he is motivated by unmet needs higher up the ladder. The need for security, having a roof over one's head and feeling safe, is the next rung. When those needs are satisfied, the person can proceed to the next rung on the ladder, the need to belong. As each need is met, the person is motivated by those needs as yet unmet. Thus, we all work toward finding fulfillment in a job or a goal, in a relationship, and in self-actualization. One is always motivated by his *unmet* needs. If you are not preoccupied with your next meal and your personal safety, you can think about other things and devote yourself to other causes. The homeless person, on the other hand, hungry and insecure, is focused on meeting those needs first. It is hard to be an activist when you cannot feed and house your family.

Many Americans, however, *are* concerned about feeding and sheltering the homeless. Communities are coming together to work on solutions to the problem. But whose

A Haitian immigrant alights from a bus under the watchful eye of a sailor before boarding a Coast Guard cutter for a return trip to Haiti.

responsibility is it to find jobs and homes for the homeless? Does a country owe its citizens shelter and food? And if you love your country and its people, what do you owe its disenfranchised?

IMMIGRANTS

Immigrants have always come to America either for greater freedom or to escape persecution or economic problems. As a matter of fact, Native Americans can rightly call us all immigrants, since they were the original inhabitants of the land.

Immigrants have invariably had trouble adjusting to their new homes. Often they are met with hostility and prejudice. The poor in the United States resented the immigrants, who suddenly were rivals for their jobs. The well-to-do resented the melting-pot mentality that saw the races blending together. Soon enough, the various immigrants groups learned to stick with "their own kind." Irish, Italians, Hispanics, and Japanese all gravitated to different parts of the city.

Immigrants have enriched America with diversity and new ideas. They have fought in America's wars, adopted its culture, and brought to it parts of their own cultures. Many older immigrants have been reluctant to "give up the old ways" because that is all they have known. It is hardest for those who left their country unwillingly. To whom do they owe allegiance? If they cherish their customs and language, are they disloyal to the country that took them in? America has not always treated its immigrants well, yet time and time again immigrants have demonstrated their loyalty by joining the armed forces to fight for their new country. Blacks fought in the American Revolutionary War, as well as the Civil War; Japanese Americans fought in World War II despite the internment of their relatives; Germans and Italians fought their countrymen helping the Allies in World War II.

Some immigrants have brought trouble and disease to the U.S. Boatloads of Cuban refugees turned out to be former prisoners and emotionally disturbed people. Crime rates soared in the overcrowded tenement conditions of Miami,

Florida, where those immigrants landed. Illegal immigrants cross the Mexican/American border daily, escaping to a supposedly better life in California and Texas.

In 1992 the United States encountered the immigrant question once again. Boatloads of Haitians, fleeing a repressive regime and an unstable economy, sailed for America, and the Coast Guard intercepted them and interned them at a U.S. naval base at Guantánamo, Cuba. When the camp was full, the government began transporting the refugees back to Haiti to face political reprisals. Some Americans charged that the United States was acting in bad faith; others held that the U.S. could not care for its own homeless, much less boatloads of immigrants. Considering that America has always been a haven for persecuted people from other lands, is it then obligated to take in all immigrants seeking asylum?

Patriotic Americans are understandably confused about the problem of the homeless and immigrants. Being proud of your country may make you want to undertake more than you're capable of accomplishing. Sometimes, as in these cases, the solutions are not easy to find.

CHAPTER 21

Patriotism and Religion

Religion has influenced people throughout the ages. It drove the Separatists to leave England for the New World; it sets immigrants apart from others almost as sharply as skin color and accent; and it became the rationale for Hitler's extermination of almost six million people. This chapter considers the question of allegiance to one's country or one's faith; since sometimes the two conflict.

The desire for a Jewish state prompted immigration to Israel; religion, therefore, drove the people back to the biblical lands to start anew. Religion also has tried to drive them out. Throughout history, Jews and Arabs have fought over the land. The Israelis feel entitled to the land of Israel, including the West Bank and Gaza, because the Bible promised it to them. The Palestinians, on the other hand, feel entitled to the land—or at least to the West Bank and Gaza—because the United Nations gave it to them when it partitioned Palestine in 1948.

Why can't these peoples get along? For the most part, it has to do with religion. Arabs and Jews owe allegiance to their faiths; their countries are extensions of those faiths. They do not believe in the same God or observe the same customs and holidays. Many do not respect the other. Each group believes that the other is trying to take something away from them.

Several wars redefined the borders originally drawn for Israel. Arabs wanted to drive the intruders out, but Israel proved surprisingly able to defend itself and added the West Bank and Gaza to its territory. The Israeli government allowed its people to settle in the occupied territories, which precipitated the Arab Intifada (or uprising) in 1987. The Palestinians, objecting to the Israeli occupation, started to fight back. Young Arabs stoned Israeli soldiers; the soldiers shot back. Arabs attacked Jews, and other Jews retaliated. The fighting continues today, neither side relinquishing its claim to the territories.

During the 1991 Gulf War, Saddam Hussein's strategy was to draw the Israelis into the fight. He rightly believed that if the Israelis fired on an Arab country, even the provocative Iraq, the other Arab countries in the coalition would withdraw. No Arab country would tolerate a Jewish attack, or even counterattack on Muslims. So Hussein aimed scud missiles at Tel Aviv, meaning to bomb Israel into reacting. To Israel's credit (and to the United States' relief), Israel did not respond, and the Arab coalition held.

The Middle East conflict goes on. New peace talks bring hope that these two peoples will find a way to live side by side harmoniously.

Religion precipitated war in Ireland, as well. In 1920, Ireland split into two parts—the largely Protestant north and the predominantly Catholic south. By 1949, the southern part of Ireland declared its independence and became known as the Republic of Ireland. Northern Ireland remained under British rule, which was abhorrent to the Catholic minority. The Protestants wanted to be ruled by the Crown, but the Catholics wanted to join the south and gain independence. Fighting broke out between the factions. Being in the majority, the Protestants held most of the power. The Catholics felt discriminated against and too few in number to change the course of events. In Belfast, barriers were erected to separate the warring sections of the city. Soon enough, Great Britain sent soldiers to Northern Ireland to restore order. The Catholics created the Irish Republican Army (IRA) to combat them, and the fighting continues today. The IRA subscribes to terrorism as a means to drive the British out of their country. People die in bombings in London and other cities. Are bombings and kidnappings "right" if committed out of religious zeal? Does winning independence or government concessions justify the killing of innocent people in both Ireland and England? Does it make moral sense to use terrorist tactics to gain religious equality any more than for political equality?

Consider again the chapter on terrorism. Many terrorists are fighting for their country, but many are fighting to protect their religious faith, as well. Khomeini and his followers were fighting for Islam; Arabs in Lebanon were fighting Jews and sometimes Christians. Is it not ironic that religious people resort to violent means to achieve a moral objective?

In both the Middle East and Ireland, children are brought up to despise their different neighbors. In Ireland, Protestants consider Catholics their born enemies even though they occupy the same country. In the occupied territories, Palestinians despise their Jewish neighbors even when they work for Jews in Israel. How does one go about healing so much hatred in the name of patriotism?

When Mohandas Gandhi had succeeded in winning India's independence from Great Britain, he discovered that the Muslim minority wanted their own country, separate from India. Thus, Pakistan was created for the Muslim Indians. Gandhi despaired that his people could not live as one country. Although he was a Hindu, he respected the other major religions and incorporated parts of each into his belief. Gandhi would have fought for the reunification of India, with religious tolerance for all, had he not been assassinated in 1948. He had demonstrated that objectives could be won with passive resistance and nonviolence; he would have used the same methods to secure religious tolerance. Instead, just before his death, he saw his people leave their homes for new ones in the "appropriate" country. Fighting even broke out between Hindus and Muslims as they passed each other on the way to and from Pakistan. It is a sad paradox that Gandhi, the great proponent of peaceful resistance, died in India's violent struggle to separate its religious groups.

People fight to defend their country from foreign invasion. They kill the enemy, and it is morally right. Sometimes, though, the enemy is their neighbor. When is a cause so "right" that children must grow up hating their countrymen?

PART VII

PUTTING IT ALL TOGETHER

CHAPTER 22

On Being a Patriot

Patriotism encompasses more than a willingness to fight for one's country. Having pride in your country means having pride in yourself. This last chapter looks at ways to cultivate and express love of country.

Loving your country means loving the land as well as the people. No better way exists to show your love for the environment than practicing conservation measures. To learn how to go about this, read the book *The Next Step: Fifty More Things You Can Do to Save the Earth*, by the EarthWorks Group. It discusses ways to conserve energy, to recycle, and to lobby your legislators, as well as organizations you can join.

Learn about your country and be proud of its accomplishments. History is important because it has a way of repeating itself. Besides your country's noble deeds, study its ignoble acts as well, so that in the future you can strive to keep similar things from happening.

After World War II, Japan made little reference in its textbooks to what really happened at Pearl Harbor. The surprise attack that drew America into the war was not something they were proud of. However, Japanese students need to know the truth of Pearl Harbor if they are to have any understanding of America's retaliation in the bombing of Hiroshima.

Textbooks in America are just beginning to reflect the country's past honestly, at long last giving credit to some of its black and women heroes, as well as admitting some of its mistakes. Someday perhaps countries such as South Africa will also begin to tell their people the truth about their history. Learning about your country's past and its relationship with other countries enables you to realize what you have, what you should strive to change, and the gifts other cultures have made to yours.

You are never too young to commit yourself to an ideal—a positive project or a goal. Join with others to seek a solution to homelessness in your community. Study the issues that affect you directly, and work toward change. What about abortion, women's rights, gay rights, and immigrant quotas, to name a few. Always be careful, though, that the groups to which you pledge your allegiance are not based on negatives. Never be swayed by hatred and bigotry; loving your country does not require you to hate some of its people.

Practice your ideals; teach them to others. In school and in the workplace, demonstrate your love for the environment. Most people learn by example; therefore, surround yourself with positive mentors and watch your own behavior. Stand up for your beliefs, but always keep an open mind. Few of us are right all the time, so it pays to be flexible.

Know your basic rights. Read your country's Constitution. If you are not aware what rights you do and do not have, how will you know how to vote in elections? Speaking of voting, register as soon as you turn eighteen and then practice your right to vote in every election thereafter. Some people think only Presidential elections are important, but the most crucial elections are often those having to do with your own neighborhood. Do not vote blindly. If you do not understand the issues, how can you vote wisely? Pick up a news magazine and read it all the way through. Listen to public radio as often as you listen to popular music stations. Encourage others to talk about issues and listen to them. The right to vote carries the obligation to be informed when you exercise that right.

When you are older, if you think you have something positive to offer your community or your country run for office yourself. If you do decide to run, base your campaign on positives, not negatives. The country does not learn much about a candidate who is intent only on disparaging his opponent.

You can join the military to demonstrate your patriotism, whether or not you actually want to bear arms. Each country owes its freedom to those who are willing to risk their lives to defend it. It takes courage to knowingly place yourself at risk, even for a good cause. But if you fight, be sure that it is for a just cause, and always uphold your convictions. Remember, even the enemy is human.

You do not have to fight in a war to show your love of country. Serving in the Peace Corps is a way to help other countries and show your patriotism at the same time.

Never be afraid to question your government. Elected officials are still human and therefore liable to err. Remember, it is your duty to challenge unjust laws. If you feel strongly enough, you may have to take to the streets. In a democracy, people have the right to protest.

Patriotism boils down essentially to one thing: giving something back to your community. In the words of the American President John F. Kennedy, "Ask not what your country can do for you; ask what you can do for your country."

FOR FURTHER READING

Aaseng, Nathan. *The Peace Seekers*. Minneapolis: Lerner Publications, Co., 1987.

Amdur, Richard. *Golda Meir*. New York: Fawcett Columbine, 1990.

Armbruster, Ann. *The American Flag*. New York: Franklin Watts, 1991.

Baines, John. *Acid Rain*. Austin: Steck–Vaughn Library, 1989.

Bryant, Adam. *Canada*. Minneapolis: Dillon Press, Inc., 1987.

Bullock, Alan. *Hitler and Stalin*. New York: Alfred A. Knopf, 1992.

Clifford, Mary Louise. *The Land and People of Afghanistan*. New York: J. B. Lippincott, 1989.

Cohen, Roger, and Gatti, Claudio. *In the Eye of the Storm*. New York: Farrar, Straus & Giroux, 1991.

Coker, Chris. *Terrorism and Civil Strife*. New York: Franklin Watts, 1987.

Cook, Fred J. *The Ku Klux Klan; America's Recurring Nightmare*. New York: Julian Messner, 1980.

Dionne, E. J., Jr. *Why Americans Hate Politics*. New York: Simon and Schuster, 1991.

Dugan, Bill. *Chief Joseph, War Chief*. New York: Harper Paperbacks 1992.

Faber, Doris and Harold. *Mahatma Gandhi*. New York: Julian Messner, 1986.

Faludi, Susan. *Backlash; The Undeclared War Against American Women*. New York: Crown Pub., 1991.

Langguth, A. J. *Patriots, The Men Who Started the American Revolution*. New York: Simon and Schuster, 1988.

Marrin, Albert. *Hitler*. New York: Viking Kestrel, 1987.

Michener, James A. *Legacy*. New York: Random House, 1987.

Ostrovsky, Victor, and Hoy, Claire. *By Way of Deception*. New York: St. Martin's Press, 1990.

Raviv, Dan, and Melman, Yossi. *Every Spy a Prince*. Boston: Houghton Mifflin Co., 1990.

Salisbury, Harrison. *Tiananmen Diary*. Boston: Little, Brown and Co., 1989.

Schwarz, Melissa. *Geronimo, Apache Warrior*. New York: Chelsea House Pub., 1992.

Smith, Betsy Covington. *Women Win the Vote*. Englewood Cliffs, NJ: Silver Burdett Press, 1989.

Smith, Samantha. *Journey to the Soviet Union*. Boston: Little, Brown and Co., 1985.

Stefoff, Rebecca. *Lech Walesa*. New York: Fawcett Columbine, 1992.

———. *Nelson Mandela*. New York: Fawcett Cloumbine, 1990.

Steins, Richard. *The Mideast After the Gulf War*. Brookfield, CT: Millbrook Press, 1992.

Ward, Geoffrey C., with Ric Burns and Ken Burns. *The Civil War*. New York: Alfred A. Knopf, Inc., 1990.

Wartik, Nancy. *The French Canadians*. New York: Chelsea House Pub., 1989.

Weiner, Eric. *The Story of Frederick Douglass, Voice of Freedom*. New York: Dell Publishing, 1992.

Wright, Robin. *In the Name of God—The Khomeini Decade*. New York: Simon and Schuster, 1989.

Yergin, Daniel. *The Prize*. New York: Simon and Schuster, 1991.

Index

Wright, Frances, 69

Y
Yeltsin, Boris, 8, 89–90

Yugoslavia, dissolution of, 90

Z
zealots, 6, 41, 46